THE FIRST MILLION

THE FIRST MILLION

BECOMING A NET **WORTH MILLIONAIRE REAL ESTATE** INVESTOR

ERIC & ERIN YOW

The First Million
Eric & Erin Yow

All rights reserved
First Edition, 2022
Copyright © 2022 Eric & Erin Yow

No part of this publication may be reproduced, stored in a retrieval system, or transmitted, in any form or by means electronic, mechanical, photocopying, or otherwise, without prior written permission of the Authors.

ABOUT THE AUTHORS

Eric & Erin Yow live, work, and play in Clarksville, Tennessee, with their two daughters, Emmalyn and Elyza. The Yows are entrepreneurs, philanthropists, small business owners, investors, and community leaders. As Christians, they have a love for the Lord and service in His name. Through all that they do, they do all to bring glory to God.

Eric is a graduate of Freed-Hardeman University and the University of Memphis School of Law. He is a practicing criminal defense attorney, as well as a real estate agent and investor. Erin is a graduate of Freed-Hardeman University and is the Executive Director of a local nonprofit.

Together, they have created the real estate investment company Yow Home Buyers, LLC, which diversifies its holdings through wholesaling, flipping, residential rental, commercial rental, land, new construction, and development. Alongside Eric's law firm, he has opened Apex Title, a real estate title and escrow company.

Eric is the founding member of the Clarksville Real Estate Investors Group. Eric & Erin teach and mentor others along their way, helping numerous people reach The First Million in their journey to success in Real Estate Investing. They both sit on the board of Yow Foundation, Inc., which strives to do good for those in need in their area.

CONTENTS

Introduction 1

Chapter 1: The Hook 5

Chapter 2: The Why 12

Chapter 3: The Wall 20

Chapter 4: The Money 33

Chapter 5: The Way 49
    Wholesaling 51
    Flipping 56
    Rentals 61
    Other Ways 73

Chapter 6: The Know 75

Chapter 7: The Deal 81

Chapter 8: The Team 99

Chapter 9: The Entity 107

Chapter 10: The Challenge 112

Chapter 11: The Dream 118

Conclusion 123

"A million dollars isn't what it used to be."

~ Howard Hughes

INTRODUCTION

As an aspiring real estate investor, you may be experiencing a handful of emotions at various times—excitement about getting started, timidity for lack of knowledge, fear of the unknown, or anxiety about when, where, and how to get started. Maybe you feel all of the above, and more, at once. It's perfectly natural and you're going to be just fine. As you study, learn, and practice, you will discover a new world, a host of hidden talents, and limits being pushed much further than you once thought possible.

Give yourself a chance to be new at this. Be willing to accept that you don't know what you don't know. You may long for the successes that other people have attained but be careful not to compare yourself to others. They are just in a different phase of the journey, or perhaps on a different journey altogether. Embrace your journey. Embrace that there will be mistakes made and problems will arise. Accept that you don't have a crystal ball and you cannot predict exactly how things will play out to the finest detail. To some degree, you've got to let go.

Key Point: Embrace your journey. Embrace that there will be mistakes made and problems will arise.

Then, take control of your future. Seize the day. Grab the bull by the horns. Make hay while the sun shines. There is a saying that the best time to invest in real estate was ten years ago and the second-best time is right now. Right now, you control what direction you move next. You determine your goals and what steps you take to advance toward them. You are the one who gets to make those decisions and—though we surely aim to help you—it is you who will be responsible for the successes you intend to enjoy. Take control.

If you want to find financial success in rental real estate, this is the book for you. With these tips and tricks, we truly can help you become a net worth millionaire. Plus, it will be much easier than you probably think. It has been said that more millionaires have been made in real estate than any other industry, and we truly believe it. The mechanism by which you can most easily grow your net worth, we contend, is by investing in real estate. The mechanism that is the most passive and with the most benefits is real estate investing. The way we first did it, and the way so many others that we have seen, met, and taught have done it, is through real estate investing.

If you think about it, most people's net worth is most directly affected by the value of their real estate minus the debt associated with it. Yes, you can work hard, save, invest in your retirement accounts, and live modestly. But if you buy a house and spend thirty years paying it off while it appreciates, compounding in value over that time, it can be a large part of one's net worth. If, however, you did that with a second home, or ten, or a hundred, or more, what then? Over time, those houses can contribute to incredible net worth and true financial freedom.

When you think about becoming a net worth millionaire, we want you to know that this is just the first benchmark in the journey. If you get in the game and play well, you'll be there before you know it. Then, the sky is the limit! What you'll soon find is that it is easier to hit that benchmark than you think. Imagine buying one rental home every six months for five years. That becomes a portfolio of ten homes from which cash flows every month, creating tax advantages for you, increasing the equity spread with every principal payment made, and appreciating automatically! Plus, if you buy *right*, you have instant equity in each home the day you bought it, which only increases over time. At some point you'll have $100,000 of equity in each home, in addition to whatever other assets you have that contribute to your net worth. Boom. Millionaire. And it wasn't even that hard.

What we think you'll find is that you may buy your first house over a period of several months, then your next will come much faster, and even faster after that. As you get better at buying, converting active projects into passive investments, and managing the people integral to the growth of your investment portfolio, you'll find that becoming a net worth millionaire happens much easier than you thought—and much faster too!

The key, then, is in getting started. Here we will teach you existing methods, specifying what worked for us and showing you *how* to get started. If you're asking "*When?*" the answer is *now*. What are you waiting for? Let's go!

Key Point: The key, then, is in getting started! Let's go!

"If you do not change direction, you may end up where you are heading."

~Lao Tzu

CHAPTER 1: THE HOOK

"Millionaire."
"A millionaire."
"That guy's a millionaire."
"I'm gonna be a millionaire."

It just rolls off the tongue, doesn't it? It's fun to say and fun to dream. A friend of ours recently remarked, "If I just had a cool million, I could really have some fun then." There's just something about that number, a million, that has its hooks in us. There's something alluring about it. It's like a checkpoint, where you will level up and everything will be different.

What is it about that number? A million. A thousand thousands. Seven figures. Why *that* number? What does it even mean to be a millionaire? To some, to become a millionaire is to reach a level of income far beyond one's contemporaries and, perhaps, to show it by living an extravagant lifestyle. To others, becoming a millionaire is just solving a math problem, one where the sum of your net worth exceeds a value of one million dollars. For the enlightened, it is the latter that holds true, as the former merely a show and a façade that can easily decay into nothingness.

If you look at all your assets; all the money you possess, the value of all the real property you own, and subtract all of your liabilities; all of your consumer debt, all of your student loan debt, your mortgage, everything, you will have a number. As clearly as 2+2=4, you can know that the number is correct. That number is—you guessed it—your Net Worth. If your net worth is equal to or greater than a million dollars, then, for our purposes, you are a millionaire. Congratulations. If not, let's go for a ride. We want to take you on a journey where you can learn just how to become a net worth millionaire through rental real estate. It is much easier than you think!

Before we get started, though, we want you to dream. Think about what you want to accomplish and truly set goals. When we are teaching real estate, or mentoring in any way for that matter, we encourage people to set goals—specifically, short term, mid-term, and long term. If you set a short-term goal, consider it to be something you want to accomplish within this calendar year or within one year, perhaps. Set a hard deadline. Mark your mid-term goals with a three-to-five year horizon. Then, we suggest your long-term goals be something like fifteen years or perhaps even all the way out to retirement, whatever that timeline looks like for you. It's okay if your goals are like someone else's, as they can be placeholders for now until you decide what you really want to do. Just set goals. You need to have something to aim for with a timeline in which to do it. If your goal is to become a net worth millionaire real estate investor, let's go!

Dream about what you could do if you could rid yourself of whatever is holding you back. Dream about what you could do if you made two times, three times, ten times what you make right now. Dream about the security you would have if you had an extra thousand dollars per month coming in as passive income. Or five thousand. Or ten. Or fifty! What could you do with that money? What could you do with your time? You probably have a scenario mapped out in your head where you could quit your day job if only you had X. If you're reading this book, you have probably already run numbers on how much cash flow in rental properties you would need in order to hit that goal. If so, let's begin. If not, dare to dream.

What if we told you that you could generate thousands of dollars in regular, passive income every month from a real estate portfolio? What if we told you that while you build that rental portfolio, you will be able to create a machine that runs day and night, weekends and holidays, working automatically to grow your net worth? Dear reader, if we can teach you how to build even a modest real estate portfolio, you will become a millionaire before you could stop to write a book about it!

Look, we don't know how you make your money right now, and that's fine. It doesn't really matter for our purposes. What we do know is that real estate has been the mechanism by which more millionaires have been made than any other source of income in existence. No matter what economic moray swept the world—whether it was the feudal times of the past, the Industrial Revolution, or even the now-ubiquitous Digital Age, real estate has always been supremely important to growing wealth. Not only that, but it has also been an egregiously necessary component of true financial growth and an incredibly reliable way to improve upon the circumstances of your birth. A famous quote by billionaire industrialist Andrew Carnegie reads, "Ninety percent of all millionaires become so through owning real estate. More money has been made in real estate than in all industrial investments combined. The wise young man or wage earner of today invests his money in real estate." It is no secret that the wealthy own real estate and real estate owners become wealthy. What's holding you back?

For a lot of people, it's all too easy to make excuses: I don't have enough money to start; I didn't start early enough; now is not the time to start investing; I don't have good luck; I have X in the way; I can't figure out where to begin. If this sounds like you, we get it. We teach our children that *can't* is a bad word—you just don't say it. Whether you think you can or you think you can't, you're right. Don't deny yourself the possibility of achieving something great just because you don't *think* you can do it. Dream. Dream big! You can do it! Let's go!

> **Key Point:** Don't deny yourself the possibility of achieving something great just because you don't *think* you can do it.

If you have breath in your lungs and the drive to become a millionaire, you can do it. If you are willing to take steps to get an education in rental real estate, you can do it. If you are prepared to shed the weight of encumbering debt and bad habits to get there, you can do it. If you are willing to sacrifice the *now*, so you can have a better *then*, you can do it. If you are willing to recreate your circle, prioritizing who you allow to influence you, you can do it. If you're ready to turn the TV off, put the phone down, and get started, you can do it!

Real estate is simply amazing. As an investment tool, there is truly no better mechanism by which to create passive income and generate a high net worth. Stocks, bonds, and mutual funds can all make you money, but there is no comparison. They may appreciate over time and even create passive income, but they are nowhere near the net worth builder that real estate can be. Financial markets are historically less stable than the real estate market and, though they are typically more liquid than real estate investments, real estate offers significantly more ways to build wealth at historically much higher returns than stocks, bonds, and mutual funds. There is simply no way to build long term wealth faster and more efficiently than by investing in real estate. Plus, it's tangible!

On this journey, though, there will be many challenges. Take the time to study. Find people you trust and learn from them. "Plans fail for lack of counsel, but with many advisors, they succeed" (Proverbs 15:22, NIV). Talk about your goals with the ones you love and surround yourself with people who will build you up. That is one of the goals of this book. Use it effectively by making it your own—write in the margins; take time to make notes; fill it with your hopes and dreams. Allow your deepest fears and your loftiest aspirations to come to life as you progress down this path. And be honest with yourself. If you know there are things or people you need to rid yourself of, write that down and take steps to do it. Your future millionaire self will thank you later.

Keep an open mind. Some of what you will read here will sound too good to be true. The pessimist within you will be quick to come up with a hundred reasons that it won't work (*e.g.,* these strategies won't work in our market; the market is too hot right now; I'd be better off waiting for the bubble to burst). But the pessimist will always be broke. It is the optimist who keeps a positive outlook, eyes on the prize, and finds ways to make it work. Speak your goals into being. Know that you can become a millionaire. Let us show you the way.

With what you'll learn here, you'll be able to get completely out of consumer debt. You'll learn to create a legitimate household budget and give yourself a raise by picking off the low-hanging fruit. You'll learn to maximize your network so that you can generate income from referral fees on deals you send to other investors. You'll learn to meet and surround yourself with other investors, such that the deals then start coming to you. You'll be able to generate leads through modern marketing, giving you the capacity to wholesale, flip, or build the rental portfolio that will be the key to becoming a millionaire—all while keeping the security of your day job in place. You'll make more money than ever and reinvest it in your portfolio, exponentially growing your holdings of cash-flowing, appreciating assets. And the systems you build along the way will allow that income and your net worth to grow into truly amazing, generational wealth.

Far faster than you think, you can become a net worth millionaire. Then, the sky is the limit! Are you hooked yet? You should be. Let's go!

THE FIRST MILLION

Notes

"Say you don't need no diamond ring and I'll be satisfied..."
~Paul McCartney

CHAPTER 2: THE WHY

But why? Why do you want to become a millionaire? If you ask a hundred people, you'll get a hundred different answers. We'll tell you ours in a moment. First, we'll say, if your *why* is because you want the comforts of life that wealth affords, if you want the big house, the fancy cars, and the lifestyle that millionaire status is assumed to provide, then you will be sorely disappointed. Genuinely, we want you to stop reading now, as this book isn't for you. If you want to become a millionaire for the joy you believe it will bring you, with weight placed in material things, it will bring nothing but pain and agony. And we don't want to teach you. Please give this book to someone else and let's part ways now.

If your *why* is more altruistic than that, "higher," if you will, then let's keep going. We want your reason to be genuine, but genuinely spiritual. This world and all that is in it is temporal, where moth and rust invariably corrupt. The list is unending of people who have pursued joy in the material yet were left wanting. You'd be a fool to think it will be different when you become a millionaire, that it will be different for you because you are different. But if you want to be wealthy for what it will allow you to do rather than what it will allow you to have, you'll be one step ahead of the game. If you want to be wealthy for how you can impact other people rather than how wealth will impact you, you're already on your way.

We want to share with you why we want to be wealthy (and why we want you to be wealthy). Know first that we have different backgrounds with different educations, life experiences, religious perspectives, and personalities. It is perfectly okay if your *why* is different from ours—we certainly are not telling you that you have to agree with us. We have been shaped by the lives we've led, as have you, and, if you think about it, the sum total of all of the decisions that we have made have brought us to these points in our lives. It would be presumptuous for us to dictate our *why* onto you. You are your own person, with your own agency and vision, so only you can decide why you want to do a certain thing.

We want to be wealthy because of what it allows us to do for other people. We are not ashamed to tell you: we are Christians. We believe in the teachings of the bible and consider it to include divine wisdom necessary to lead a truly fulfilling life. That said, we do not live our lives for ourselves. We live for Him, who died for us. In service to Him, He has authority over everything about us and everything in our lives. His Word has taught us to use our abilities to serve the Lord and be a blessing to those around us. We want to be wealthy because wealth is how we can better contribute to the church, how we can better provide for our family, and how we can be a bigger blessing to our community.

We are thankful that God has put us in a position in this life where we can have good jobs, run successful businesses, and build an investment portfolio that has grown a net worth that we never imagined possible. We know that God is to credit, for every good thing comes from Him. We are thankful to Him because He has entrusted us with so much, with an expectation that we would be good stewards of these blessings. As we continue to steward them well, He has continued to entrust. We fully believe that if we took our eyes off of the Lord, it could all be taken away in a moment's time!.

We want to be a blessing to those around us. We want to be able to provide for those who cannot provide for themselves. We want to be so magnificently wealthy that there is nothing we couldn't do to bless people in the name of the Lord. We want to send other people's children to college. We want to pay off the widow's house. We want to be able to give away houses and build hospitals. If this is how the Lord will use us, we want to do it. This is our *why*. It is what drives us.

So we are clear, we do not love money, though. We simply love the good that money allows you to do in His name! Imagine your neighbor has an emergency and they need $10,000 right now. You really want to help, but you weigh that desire against your own needs and wants. You may even have that money to give, but there is a burden in knowing the other ways you could be using that money. Maybe you have your own bills that need to be paid. Maybe you are afraid to deplete your own emergency funds; what if you have an emergency? You'd hate to miss a car payment. What about that thing you were saving up to buy? You already know they can't possibly pay you back, so that money would be gone forever. You give them $100, pray that others chip in enough to save the day, and move on, keeping the nagging feeling that you wish you could have done more.

What if you could have done more? What if you were consumer-debt free, your income was more than enough to cover your household budget (because you live responsibly, below your means), and you have been wise in your saving? Perhaps because of this prudence, you've created significant monetary gain, growing your accounts and investing in appreciating assets that have put you in a strong financial position. Moreover, because you have cultivated your network in order to surround yourself with people who are a positive influence on your life, you are connected with many others who are similarly successful and similarly charitably minded. You could pick up the phone and call on any number of people who could help out and donate to the cause. You pick up a pen and write a check for exactly what your neighbor needs.

We want to be there for our neighbor. We want to have the financial freedom that permits us to do the greatest good for the greatest number of people, spreading the love of God in unimaginable ways. This is our motivation to push ourselves further and further. This is our *why*. We know that God doesn't need *our* money—it's His anyway. He needs *us*. He has us. And if He blesses us with financial gain, He can have that too!

Our journey began with the intense desire to get out of debt and get that massive weight off our backs. When we met, we became fast friends, dated, and fell in love. Upon marrying one another, forever joining our two distinctly separate lives together into one, it became one of our most important shared goals to get ourselves out of debt. We wanted to start a family on a different financial track than what we had had as children. We were determined that the only way we would be able to get ahead was to dominate our debt and make choices that aligned with the financial future to which we aspired. This meant giving up the prospect of some shiny, new things. It meant budgeting hard. It meant getting an education in debt reduction and implementing strategies to get out of debt as fast as possible. Then, we began investing in business, real estate, and our financial futures. We began striving to put ourselves in a better position, so when our neighbor calls, we will be there.

It is apparent that many people want to be rich because of the things it allows them to be able to afford—big houses, nice clothes, fancy cars, expensive jewelry, lavish vacations, and so on. When a young person from a modest upbringing gets a multi-million-dollar contract playing sports, it is no surprise that he or she buys the "shiny, new things" we mentioned. It is also not surprising when that same person files for bankruptcy later. We contend that if you want to be rich so that you have riches, you will be poorer than ever before, never truly satisfied with the shiny, new things. As trite as it may sound—money cannot buy happiness. Money can, however, allow you to bless other people in a way that brings amazing joy to the recipient and the giver. The Savior put it this way, "it is more blessed to give than to receive," and it is true indeed.

> **Key Point:** If you want to be rich so that you have riches, you will be poorer than ever before.

If you struggle with materialism, spend a few dollars and read Rabbi Harold Kushner's book *When All You've Ever Wanted Isn't Enough*. It is life changing. Also, read the wisdom of Solomon in the bible book of Ecclesiastes, where he likens materialism unto chasing after the wind, calling it vanity and profitless. There, the author recalls his earlier life in which he did more and more, trying to find some satisfaction in the accomplishments or activities of the day. At the time, he was pleased with the fruit of his labor, and, being pleased, at the time, was his reward. But "…behold all was vanity and striving after wind and there was no profit under the sun." This lays bare an important lesson for all times, whether biblical or modern. Material joy fades. True joy lies elsewhere.

You could pursue wealth for wealth's sake. You may even become wealthy, doing so to find joy in material things. But what you will quickly realize is that there is no real joy in these physical things.

We want your *why* to be for something greater. Something much greater. We want you to aspire to higher ideals and to want to be wealthy, if that is the path you choose, so that you can make a huge difference in your community. Long to be wealthy so that you can build a homeless shelter in your city. Work to grow your portfolio so that you can give a house to someone in need one day. Dream of making such a donation that a children's hospital can build a new wing, expanding their capacity to do good to so many who are in need. Dream big. Think of something awesome and good in scope—which you'd never be able to do if you're broke—and let *that* be your drive to be successful. Find your *why* in something that has a higher purpose, transcending the temporal, material things presently just outside your grasp.

If your *why* is a fast car, it will never be fast enough. If it is a big house, it will never be big enough. If your *why* is self-centered, you will never be satisfied with the results, and you should stop reading this book altogether. We do not want to help you get rich merely so you'll have personal, financial gain. We aim not to enable any sort of selfish materialism. You need a new, higher reason to become wealthy. Only by doing this, and consciously choosing to bring your life in accordance with whatever God's plan may be for you, will you be able to find an undeniable reason to start your journey. Pray for wisdom. Then, it is time to begin. And, we believe it will come faster and easier than you think.

THE FIRST MILLION

Notes

"How to make a million dollars: First, get a million dollars."

~ Steve Martin

CHAPTER 3: THE WALL

As we prepare for this journey, we want to get on the same page about something. It is not especially hard to become a net worth millionaire, as we keep saying. But what does that even mean? A lot of people confuse the concept of net worth with that of income, so we want to help you understand and be able to differentiate between the two. Your income is the amount of money you have coming in a given period. Your net worth, on the other hand, is simply a representation of how strong your financial position is. Calculating it is fairly straightforward, as we mentioned before: Net worth = assets - liabilities. Assets are things you own which possess some calculable value. Liabilities are the debt you have on those or other things.

Let's understand net worth with a simple calculation. Say you own a $150,000 house, a $25,000 car, and $25,000 cash. You owe $140,000 on the house, $30,000 on the car, $20,000 in consumer debt, and $90,000 in student loans. A simple net worth calculation would go something like this: Assets ($150,000+25,000+25,000) – Liabilities

($140,000+30,000+20,000+90,000) = a Net Worth of −$80,000. You read that correctly if you read *negative* eighty thousand dollars. That figure means that you will need to acquire an additional $80,000 just to break even!

Yikes, right? Although this is an over-simplified version of how to calculate your net worth, it exposes you to the single most obvious truth in the world of money: debt is a dream killer. More specifically, debts like student loans and consumer debts are dream killers. They can linger on for decades if you let them, forcing you to put your aspirations on the backburner as time marches on—*your* time. Student loans, in particular, are very rarely forgiven, and defaulting on either of these types of debt can seriously ruin your credit, making your financial dreams much more difficult to realize. If you want to have a million-dollar net worth, you've got to get out from under the weight of consumer and student loan debt.

However, if these debts are so debilitating, you may wonder why not get out of all debt? Well, that's another conversation to have entirely. Debt is a tricky subject, with differing opinions across the board. It really depends on your philosophy toward debt, which we will get into later at a much deeper level. Once you have educated yourself on the subject, you are in a position to make an informed decision about how to approach debt. If you decide to be totally debt averse, you will begin by paying off all of your student loans, consumer debt, your house, and any other debts before you begin investing in real estate. Then, as you begin investing, you'll want to save enough liquid capital to buy your investment properties free and clear.

While that may sound like a safe way to do things, it will not only take longer but also afford you no guarantees that it will get you where you want to be. You may run the risk of falling victim to the fallacy of sunk costs—the compulsion to continue doing what you've put significant time into simply because you've put time into it. If you walk your path at a slower pace, you may run the risk of believing that's the only way you should go because you've been doing it for a while. This may sap you of your entrepreneurial drive and cause you to miss out on opportunities. You may also, literally, run out of time.

However, if you decide to be more discerning, espousing the position that there is good debt and bad debt, things take a different route. First off, you will get rid of all of your *bad debt* as quickly as possible. Then, as you begin investing, you'll maintain the discipline of acquiring assets using *good debt* and thereby increase your net worth, using leverage to generate a higher return on your investment. This not only forces you to take a good hard look at your life and seek out real, meaningful change but also enables you to seek and find incredible opportunities for growth.

> **Key Point:** Get rid of your bad debt as soon as possible!

So, where do you begin? Volumes have been written about the subject of getting out of debt, and there are several proven strategies you could employ. The most important fact is that you need to get your head right first. Debt doesn't just magically show up at our doorstep. We all have some spending quirks or issues which lead us down the rabbit hole until we find ourselves totally buried. If your issue is credit cards, for instance, even if someone came along and paid off all of your cards for you, it wouldn't change anything. You would go back to your old ways and rack up even greater credit card debt, until one day you found yourself in the same position, only to realize that your issue is still the way you use credit cards.

True change requires true grit. You've got to commit to the plan by changing your spending habits. It's simple. To get out of credit card debt, you've got to stop using credit cards! You have to identify the issues and correct them. Do you shop for reasons other than utility? Perhaps you resort to *retail therapy* instead of dealing with your stress in a healthy manner? Maybe you have compulsions you don't yet understand or memories of mistakes of which you haven't let go. Whatever it is, you need to get to the root of your habits, because no amount of money can ever fix them. Get your head wrapped around your inner self and you will see the burdens that have been weighing you down. Then, when you are ready, surrender your financial habits to God. Once your spiritual affairs are in order, you will find the inner strength you need to manifest true, positive change in your life. You will be ready to get out of debt.

When we first aimed to get out of debt, we studied the writings of Dave Ramsey. You can research him or look into other debt-reduction methods, choosing the ones that you believe will work the best for you. Learn the method you choose through and through. Make a plan. Then, follow the plan, committing to the goal of eradicating your debt. We talk about Ramsey because that is what worked for us and we would like to share the insights we gleaned after much trial and error.

Ramsey's plan is simplified into a number of steps he calls "baby steps," because each step functions as a small part of the larger scheme. To start off on your debt reduction journey, Dave suggests you save up for a small, starter emergency fund. Next, pay off all of your consumer debt except your primary residence's mortgage, using what he calls the Debt Snowball®. Then, grow your emergency fund until it contains an amount equivalent to 3-6 months of your monthly expenses. Only then does he suggest making investments, with the next steps dealing with investing for the future, paying off your home's mortgage, and working to build wealth.

If you were to ask for our oversimplified version of how to get out of debt, so that we don't have to spend a hundred pages talking about it, here's what it would be: First things first, you simply must get a household budget together. Long before you even look at investing or begin paying down your debts, know what your money is doing right now. We cannot stress how crucial this is.

When we have been negligent about our habits for years, an exaggerated blind spot develops, making it hard to be objective about our financial strengths and weaknesses. Therefore, you must begin your debt eradication journey with an honest inventory of your household. If you've never done a budget before, this will take several attempts over the course of several months, because you'll be refining and fine-tuning your numbers as you see what money is coming in and where it is going. Maybe you'll discover that your seemingly innocent $5 coffees have been adding up to a shocking amount. You'll begin changing your habits once you see them laid out in front of you in black and white.

An effective way to do this is to utilize the data tracking services provided by your bank. Get online and pull up your primary checking account. Presumably, this is where your paychecks go in and your expenses go out. Print the last six full months of statements so that you can look at each line item and get deep in the weeds with it. Yes, we know there are programs and websites that can do this for you, but there is something to be gained by spending a few hours writing down exactly where you are spending your money (You probably got here through negligence and lack of awareness, remember? True reckoning requires deliberate, conscious intent.)

If you use credit cards, pull up the same six months of statements for them as well. Get a yellow pad (or spreadsheet) and make columns for each expense, writing out exactly what you have spent every dollar on. You'll have a column for fuel, for instance, so in that column write down every dollar you've spent on fuel for six months. You could do three months, but six months gives you a better average. If you're bold, have the time, and really want to atone for your financial misadventures, go back a year!

When you are done, we want you to have every dollar you have spent assigned to a column, with no exceptions. Total those columns, then divide by six to get your average. If you remember things you pay for annually, include those, divided by twelve. You'll know with a high degree of probability what you'll spend on various things, like fuel, in the next month.

Use those columns' headings to create budget line items, no matter how trivial, because, on average, you spend one-sixth of the total you added up. As you put your budget together, you'll be able to see very quickly where you can cut some spending. It will be a beautiful thing and a huge victory early in the game for you to start to make changes in your spending habits. Then, as we talk about getting you out of debt, your budget will become your best friend.

When working on a budget, most people focus on the "income" side and think it is the key to saving, getting out of debt, and providing for one's financial future. We cannot tell you the number of times we have heard people say, "If I just had a better job or could get a raise, I could fix my budget." The problem is that if you increase the income side, you're probably going to increase the spending side to further improve your standard of living. You'll see the extra money and feel you can afford those shiny new things you had been putting off purchasing. This is only human. Plus, it might be hard or take a long time to find a higher paying job or get that raise you want.

Instead, you should first focus on the "expenses," where you can give yourself an immediate raise by cutting some of the spending. Yes, you heard that right. Expenses spared is income gained! If you spend $50 going through the coffee shop drive through each month, cutting that in half immediately gives you a $25 per month raise. Making coffee at home may save you even more. If you spend hundreds of dollars each month eating out, buy groceries and eat at home—investing some time improving your cooking will save you a lot of those hard-earned dollars. Additionally, you'll gain a new skill that you can show off to impress your friends and prospective clients!

Your budget will reveal the impact of your wasteful and expensive indulgences, such as smoking cigarettes or drinking alcohol. We want you to spend the time to calculate how much you would save if you quit altogether. We promise you it'll be shocking once you've added the figures up. The money you save on the expenses side can be easy money!

> **Key Point:** Your budget will shed light on how you are actually spending your money.

Some items on the expenses side will require a bit more work, but not to worry. If you make a game out of it, it can be a lot of fun to find creative ways of minimizing those numbers. Keeping the big picture in mind, with the goal of getting you out of debt and onto becoming a net worth millionaire in rental real estate, you will make some sacrifices, for sure. But some of those sacrifices will come easy, knowing that making them is totally worth it.

Consider your car note, for instance. If you are driving a car worth $25,000, that you owe $30,000 on because you just had to have that shiny, new thing, you can see how counterproductive this is to improving your financial position. You just have to be willing to sacrifice and be a little creative. In the case of the shiny car, you could continue to pay on your note, say $600 per month, until it is paid off. Or you could sell it, using cash to make up the difference, and buy a much cheaper car to drive. It may be unfortunate that you're upside down on the car at the moment, but staying upside down on it for years would definitely be worse, especially if it kept you from being able to invest those dollars in your financial future. This very real expense is called *opportunity cost*. The opportunity cost of that car is a lot more than the $5,000 spread. It is the amount of time that you are bogged down by this amount. And time is too precious of a resource to be squandered.

We'll propose one solution worth considering—sell the car. Even if you had to come up with $5,000 to make up the difference, selling the car immediately eliminates $600 per month in expenses off your budget. You could then spend a little money to get a beater just to get you around until you could afford (or justify) something more expensive. Be willing to think outside the box. Even if you just downsized to a $10,000 car that you owe $15,000 on because of the mistake of buying the first vehicle, cutting your $600 monthly payment down to a $300 payment frees up that money on the expenses side. Remember your *why* and have faith. You can do it!

We call this concept, *finding money*. Go through every line item on the expenses side of your budget and play the same game over and over, asking "how can I reduce this?" Are you brave enough to cut out cable TV and watch recordings of your favorite shows online, even if that means falling behind everybody in the neighborhood by a few weeks? Are you strong enough to cancel your gym membership and use free fitness apps to train yourself at home? Are you committed enough to forego some of the things you want to spend money on so that you can free up that money on the expenses side in order to get you closer to the goal?

Be bold. Don't be afraid to call your debtors and ask if they'll take fifty cents on the dollar to pay off the debts in full more quickly. Shop around for insurance quotes and find something cheaper than what you have now. Go with a cheaper cell phone carrier, even if that means you have to change phone numbers or incorporate more VoIP services in your life. Get creative. See how much money you can *find* in your own budget. Find as much as you can and do it every month. Then, as you cut your frivolous spending, maintain disciplined spending habits, and have your eyes focused on the goal, your budget will be the springboard you need to start paying off all of your debts.

If you want to become a net worth millionaire investing in real estate, the wall you've got to overcome first is that debt. Whether you use Dave Ramsey's Debt Snowball® or some other method, you've simply got to attack the debt. In the Debt Snowball® method, you chart all of your debts in descending order by balance, irrespective of monthly payment amount or interest rate. Keep making minimum payments on all debts except the one with the lowest remaining balance. That one you work to pay off as quickly as possible. Having paid off the debt with the lowest remaining balance, you then move to paying off the next lowest. This creates a snowball effect, where the money you would have been using to make the payment on the lowest payment, now paid off, begins paying on the next lowest. You'd continue this strategy until all of your debts have been paid off, with the exception of your primary residence.

Another strategy you could employ is to chart your debts by the interest rate accruing against you, paying off the highest interest rate debts first and working your way down to the lowest interest rate. While the snowball strategy helps build momentum faster, this method has merit because the dollar simply goes further as you reduce principal balances on higher interest rate accounts. Take some time to run the numbers on both strategies, using your actual debts and what you think works best for you. Make an educated decision on how to attack your debts, then attack them with all of your might. For us, the snowball was the fastest way to build momentum, a factor which outweighed the cost of waiting to pay down the higher interest rate debts.

Next, we want to introduce you to a concept we call "Debt Domination." When we are teaching people how to get out of debt, we always go through the budget process first, as above, so that we can lean hard into this new concept. Debt Domination is the mindset first and then the practice of using every dollar you could possibly find and spend on dominating that debt. If you want to get out of debt fast, Debt Domination is the bolt of lightning you need to ride to get there. Every dollar that you *find* in your budget, use it to hammer the debt with the lowest remaining balance.

> **Key Point:** Every dollar that you *find* in your budget, use it to hammer the debt with the lowest remaining balance.

If you can find change in your couch cushions, use it to hammer that debt. If you can sell some of your stuff, downsize your apartment or car, put in overtime at work, or pick up a second job, use it to hammer that debt. If you use every dollar you could possibly find to attack your debts, it will be amazing to you how fast you can become debt free. It is truly exhilarating and addictive. Then, to be able to shed that weight that keeps you from running toward your goals will bring an unbelievable feeling of relief. That alone will make this process worthwhile.

But you cannot merely dive headfirst into paying off your debts. Remember when I mentioned getting your head right first? If you don't address your financial propensities, you'll just wind up back in the same position you were in. Hugely important: if credit is part of the problem, stop using credit cards! Do this: fund your emergency fund and only use it for emergencies. Stop buying things on credit, period! Call and cancel your credit cards. Cut up the cards and never look back. You can cancel the card even with a balance on the account.

Just pay it off as part of your Debt Domination and never put yourself in that position again!

By the time you have overcome "The Wall" of your debt, you will have refined and fine-tuned your budget countless times. With this comes an unexpected and pleasant surprise—increased financial literacy! You will get quite good at math, if you weren't already. That is equivalent to unlocking a superpower! You will have a good foundation for a very important component of your education in real estate investing—numbers. Numbers are everything. Get your practice in with your budget and Debt Domination, then the rest of the math, and the journey, will come easy.

Notes

"Money is only a tool. It will take you wherever you wish, but it will not replace you as the driver."

~Ayn Rand

CHAPTER 4: THE MONEY

One of the most common questions we get asked about real estate investing is "how much money do I need to get started?" There is a misconception that in order to become wealthy investing in real estate you must already be wealthy. The notion that "it takes money to make money" is certainly true, but there is a lot of misinformation out there about what it takes to become a real estate investor. If you look around, you'll find books and teachers professing that you can, and perhaps should, invest with no money down, risking zero dollars of your own capital. But you'll also find people who say you should have tens or hundreds of thousands to invest before you get started so you have the cushion, equity, and cash flow that comes with big down payments and lower debt.

Let me clear something up—the money is not the hard part. Without a doubt, *finding the deal* is the hardest part of investing in real estate. Becoming a net worth millionaire real estate investor is almost automatic once you solve these two problems: finding the deal and funding the deal. If you can find the deal, you can find the money. What that looks like will vary from deal to deal and person to person, but in this chapter we will explore how to fund your venture into real estate investing. We hope this chapter will serve as a bit of encouragement as you gear up for the hunt, too. At the end of the day, funding the deal is not as hard as you may think.

> **Key Point:** The money is not the hard part.

The most common type of funding is through a conventional bank. The traditional banking route is often considered the first place to look for money because it is within reach of most people. You probably pass a dozen banks on the way to work in the morning, each with their well-lit marquees advertising their lowest rates and latest promotions. It is easy to call a bank, make a fast-friend over the phone, build a relationship with the lender that suits you best, and apply for any number of banking products that a bank wants, and needs, to lend you. You could also find competitive rates by comparing national lenders online or, if you want to stay local, shopping your loan to mortgage brokers in your area. Remember, if you have imperfect credit and need a smaller down payment, you will probably be shopping for government insured or guaranteed loans (e.g. FHA, VA, USDA).

Often called a conventional loan, you can apply for it with as much as a thirty-year term with a low fixed rate, which, if you own your primary residence, you have probably already done before. The beauty of a conventional loan is the relatively low interest rate you can lock in for a long period of time over which to pay it off. There are downsides to consider, though, as you may be limited to a certain number of conventional loans.

The process to apply for a conventional loan is substantially more difficult, as well. There are a lot more hoops to jump through and the process takes a bit longer, often putting you at a disadvantage in a time-sensitive transaction. In a competitive market, when you must make an offer contingent upon conventional financing, it is much less attractive to a seller than an offer without such a contingency.

There's a workaround to this, though. The same bank you called for a conventional loan likely has a commercial lending department. In commercial lending, especially with smaller community banks, there is a shot-caller who can decide whether to lend to an applicant. Even if that shot-caller has to present the prospect loan to their board of directors, there will clearly be a decision-maker at hand, with authority to lend, without having to get you to jump through the hoops present in conventional financing. Build a relationship with that person and you'll be in great shape to bag attractive deals.

While your local bank generally sells your conventional loan to another bank, acting primarily as the broker during the application process, a commercial loan would typically stay in-house. This creates an advantage in that you continue to deal with the same bankers and tellers over time, further building that relationship. When you need another loan, it's easy to call on the same people who have helped you so many times before, who smile at you when you come in to make a payment or deposit, laugh at your jokes, and are thankful for your business. I absolutely love some of the local banks and bankers we deal with on a weekly basis, and I could not imagine going forward without them!

Commercial loans have generally shorter terms with adjustable rates. For instance, you may get a five-year term loan, meaning the rate will adjust at the end of that five-year term but the payment will be amortized over a longer term, usually fifteen, twenty, or even twenty-five years. You should expect to put down about 20%, but you may find banks who are willing to accept as little as 10% down on the purchase and still finance all of the repairs the home needs. We will get into the numbers later, but you should familiarize yourself with these concepts early. For instance, shorter amortization means higher payments with more being paid toward principal. Longer amortization means early payments are comprised of more interest and less principal, but the payments are lower. Longer amortization means higher cash flow, while shorter amortization means quicker pay-off. Your goals will dictate which you choose.

Adjustable rate loans or term loans often scare investors, since the rate is not locked into place for the life of the loan. As interest rates fluctuate with the rise and fall of the financial markets, you could be in for a surprise when the bank raises your rate at the end of the term. At that point, the rental where cash flowed well may no longer provide excess or may even now have a negative cash flow with the higher monthly payment. However, a well-studied and prudent investor knows that the market has remained relatively stable over time and will lock in when rates are low, even with the occasional refinance. Lock in the best rate for the longest period and you'll increase your chances for long-term success.

Some of you may want to buy on revolving lines of credit because of the speed at which you can move using that funding source as if it were cash. Or you may purchase in cash and then, instead of another financing mechanism, you refinance the subject property by putting a line of credit against it. These are great because payments are not amortized and your interest-only payments create significantly better cash flow than their amortized counterparts. Lines of credit, though, usually have especially short terms, even just one or two years. So, your interest rate, terms, and loan are only locked in for potentially twelve months, with a cost associated with renewing it at expiration.

One danger in short term loans like a revolving line of credit is that at the end of the term, the full balance is due in full if it is not renewed. Whether or not it gets renewed is not an assumption you'll want to make in a volatile market, because it is the bank that gets to decide whether or not it wants to keep that kind of loan—or that kind of client—on the books. The bank may decide because of a downturn in the market, poor payment history, or other circumstances that affect you or your loan, that your line of credit is too risky. If the bank chooses not to renew, you may be in a tricky spot trying to reposition, especially if other banks have similarly tightened up.

But the likelihood is probably low that a bank will simply cut you off, especially if you are a strong, quality client of the bank, have money on deposit, and always make payments on time. From the bank's perspective, it makes more sense to have a performing loan earning them interest from a client who always pays on time, secured by an asset worth more than the debt it covers, than to not renew it. However, if the client is a risk to them, the asset is insufficient to secure the debt (perhaps because of a recession or crash), and the money loaned could be better performing elsewhere in their portfolio, the decision could be made not to renew. So, build strong relationships, pay on time, and make the bank money. If you make the bank money, they'll love you for it and keep lending to you. When you have banks that *want* to loan you money, real estate investing can really come easy.

One strategy we have employed with our local banks is to use a line of credit to make purchases and then cash-out refinances to put debt on the asset and pay off the line of credit. If you have a home with equity in it, you may have, or at least have heard of, a home equity line of credit, often called a HELOC. A home equity line of credit is exactly what it sounds like. It is a line of credit with a bank that is secured by the equity in your home. If you own a home worth $200,000 but you owe $100,000 on it, you could go to your bank and ask for a line of credit against the equity in your home. Most banks would extend up to 80% (or more!) loan-to-value, or as much as $160,000, minus the $100,000 first position mortgage, leaving you a $60,000 equity position with which you could obtain a line of credit.

> **Key Point:** When banks want to loan you money, real estate investing becomes much easier!

With a line of credit, you use it like a bank account—pull money out when you need it, leave it there when you don't. As you pull money out to invest in real estate (not go on trips or by shiny things) you will incur interest on the debt. When you pay the line of credit off or leave it at a zero balance, it costs you nothing in interest. The beauty of a line of credit is that you can make cash offers on real estate without having actual cash in the bank or a sock drawer. You can close in a matter of days simply by going to the teller and requesting a cashier's check against the line of credit. Sellers like cash and fast closings! Lines of credit give you the speed and efficiency it takes to be competitive in real estate.

A home equity line of credit is secured by your home, which means that if you sold your home you would have to pay off the line of credit as well as the first position mortgage. If you defaulted on the line of credit, your home would be at risk for foreclosure. Many would advocate that you should never put your primary residence at risk by using a home equity line of credit to invest in real estate. Doing so creates a vulnerable position for you and your family, because if things went south, they could go very, very wrong. It can be done safely, but if you are already in a strained financial position, we would not increase the risk by using a home equity line of credit as the source of funding.

An unsecured line of credit is a different animal, but it works very much the same. You often need a strong financial position or sufficient income sources to be able to acquire an unsecured line of credit at a bank. Since the line of credit is not secured by real estate on which the bank could foreclose in the event of default, it is harder to recover and is therefore considered one of the riskier lending strategies that a bank would consider. However, to a strong, dependable client, a bank will extend these unsecured lines of credit. One strategy is to build a relationship with your bank or banks, prove yourself to be dependable by borrowing and repaying, keep money (e.g., your primary checking or savings accounts) on deposit with them, then test the water by asking for a small unsecured line of credit. Over time, you may be able to increase the amount of that line of credit as you prove your worth to the bank.

With a line of credit, you could flip a house by buying with "cash" and renovating with funds from that line, saving the additional expense that financing it would incur. Then you would sell the house for a profit and simply pay back the line of credit and do it again. Rinse and repeat. Or, if you are purchasing a rental home, the line of credit gives you the capacity to buy the house, renovate as needed, and then refinance it. Our favorite strategy is to use a line of credit to buy the rental house and immediately take it to a bank at which we can get a commercial loan. They'll often refinance it in as little as three to four weeks, provided our renovations are nearly complete. That refinance is usually as much as seventy-five or eighty percent of the appraised value, generally more than enough to cover the balance owed on the line of credit. This strategy is amazing because it allows us to be zero-down in a rental house that is rented and cash flowing in as little as a month!

Looking at an example, we recently capitalized on an opportunity to acquire a home for $100,000 that needed about $24,000 in renovations to make it rent ready. We purchased it with a line of credit and immediately initiated a refinance. By the time we closed and had it refinanced, the debt incurred was about $128,000 on a house that appraised for $170,000. The bank loaned us about $128,000 on a commercial refinance with a five-year term and twenty-year amortization. The home very quickly rented at $1350 per month, making this a great deal on a cash-flowing property where we had exactly zero dollars of our own money invested. This funding mechanism is absolutely brilliant!

This strategy is often called the BRRRR method, and we love it. You Buy the property, Renovate it, Rent it, and Refinance your money back out so you can Repeat the process over and over again.

Buy, Renovate, Rent, Refinance, and Repeat.

Buy, Renovate, Rent, Refinance, and Repeat.

If you want to become a net worth millionaire investing in real estate, the BRRRR method is an incredible strategy. And don't worry if you don't have a line of credit to do it with—there are other funding sources out there worthy of discussion.

Perhaps you've heard of personal loans, private money, or hard money-lenders. A lot of people get their start in real estate investing by first talking to their friends and family about what they want to do. No one likes asking for money, but if you have a rich uncle, you would be silly not to at least talk to him about what you are getting ready to do. He may shoot you down, but he may love the idea of diversifying his portfolio or making more money by lending than he can make putting it in a Certificate of Deposit. If he's making two percent in a money market account, offer him ten percent interest on a loan secured by a great piece of real estate and he may love you for the opportunity.

In general, personal loans are loans made from person to person, ordinarily with a prior relationship. You always want terms in writing, signed by both parties, even though—and perhaps especially—it is family. Personal loans are an easy way to get started because your friends and family often want to support you or help you along your journey. If you can prove you are educating yourself in real estate investing and you've found a deal worth jumping on, the personal loan may be the easiest way to get it done.

Private money loans, sometimes called hard money, work the same way personal loans do, where you borrow a certain amount of money on terms. However, it's a bit more at an arms-length basis lacking the familial relationship between the parties. Private money lenders want to know you can repay the loan, that the loan is secured by a strong asset (e.g., a flip with sizable profit margins or a rental property with equity), and that they will make good money on the loan. When borrowing private money, expect to pay a higher interest rate and origination fee, with a shorter term (six months is common) and balloon payment at the end of the term. It will cost more than a commercial bank loan but it may be easier to acquire. These lenders accept a bit more risk but you pay for it in interest and fees.

With private lenders, you may be able to negotiate terms such as no payments for six months or interest-only payments during the term of the loan. If you are flipping, it is nice not to have to make payments on the loan, then just pay it off when you sell the home for a profit! If you are trying to BRRRR, using hard money is an expensive, but accessible, short term loan you can use to make quick purchases, then refinance with your bank to pay off the hard money loan. You could use this method until you have enough in savings to be your own lender, borrowing from your own cash reserves to buy the home to flip or rent and refinance. Educate yourself on each of these strategies and use what works best for you.

There are also a number of financing options under the umbrella term of *creative financing*, often simply called seller financing. If a homeowner owns a house free and clear, it is a beautiful thing to be able to negotiate financing terms directly with them. Perhaps the seller wants all cash with a fast closing and will cut you a deal so they can cash out quickly. Perhaps the seller doesn't want a lump-sum payment but needs monthly income without the headaches of having to rent the property out. They may be willing to accept even a zero-percent interest with a small down payment and reasonable monthly payments spread out over ten years or so. You can really get creative with sellers who own a home free and clear. Find out what they want and see what options you can create that help them reach their goals while you move toward yours.

Even if a seller doesn't own the home free and clear, you can still get creative. There is a method of buying houses subject to the existing mortgage balance, which is the exclusive investing strategy of some who invest in single family residential homes. There are a number of ways to do it, whether in your own name, in an LLC, or with a Trust device. Generally speaking, a seller agrees to sell you the property but leave the existing mortgage in place in their name. You, the buyer, agree to pay the mortgage until it is paid off, whether at the end of the term or when you sell the property and the note must be satisfied. This strategy is fraught with difficulty, complicated legal documents, and risks, but if you educate yourself well, it can be an extraordinary mechanism and another tool in your tool belt.

While this is not our primary investing strategy, it is nice to know how "sub-to" arrangements work so that you can recognize an opportunity when you see one. It may not make sense to purchase a home the traditional route, due to closing costs and finance charges. The homeowner may owe more on their loan than the sale would satisfy or perhaps the house needs repairs they cannot afford to make. You can create margins or offer a better sale price to the seller by offering to purchase the home subject to the existing mortgage. If their rate and terms are substantially better than what you would get if you obtained traditional financing, it would be significantly beneficial to you. Their loan is probably a thirty-year fixed rate at a low interest rate. If you financed the new purchase on a commercial loan, you would spend thousands in closing costs and fees only to have a shorter term and higher interest rate. Leaving their loan in place may make an otherwise bad deal into a viable one, so educate yourself on how to analyze these.

There are risks and downsides to buying homes "subject-to" for both the seller and the buyer. However, while none are insurmountable, they should give you a reason to pause and plan. Do not become enamored with the idea and rush in without sufficient education on the strategy. For instance, the seller's mortgage terms have a "Due on Sale" clause that is triggered when you purchase the home. There are ways to avoid the mortgagor calling the note due, like having the seller place the home in trust, naming their self as beneficiary and trustee. Then, they name you as beneficiary and resign as trustee, naming you as successor trustee. You then own the home, as beneficiary of the trust, and the mortgage stays in place in the name of the seller. Naming the trust something like "*Seller's Name* Family Trust" helps obscure the fact that the property has changed hands. This strategy has always struck us as sneaky and leaves a sour taste in our mouths. But it clearly works, and some investors use this strategy exclusively.

One risk is to the seller, in a subject-to scenario. Once you have closed on it, they are in a seriously vulnerable position. For one thing, it stays on their balance sheet and detrimentally affects their debt-to-income ratio, which could preclude them from buying their next home. If you lack the requisite ethic to make absolutely certain that payments are made every time, on time, the seller is at risk of having their credit harmed. If you fell on hard times and had to miss a payment, the seller is the one whose credit suffers. If you are trying to rent the home but it sits vacant and you do not have the means to keep the payment current, the seller is the one who will get foreclosed on—not you. If the lender forecloses on a home that you now own and, worse yet, have sold to a tenant buyer on a rent to own contract or wrap around mortgage, it will be months or years of litigation and thousands upon thousands in attorneys' fees to unravel the deal. The seller's financial position would be irreparably harmed and, when their aggressive plaintiff's lawyer sues you for your misdeeds, it could ruin you.

Scared yet? You should be. Just enough to be cautious. Do not buy a house subject to the existing mortgage until you know how to do it properly and can ensure that you can see the deal through to the end.

We own properties that we have purchased subject to the existing mortgage and will do it again when it is the right way to approach a given deal. We have studied the best ways to execute the subject-to model and are convinced that were anything to go sideways down the line, we could simply refinance the home and pay off the existing debt. We have heard other investors say they love the subject to model because the debt is not in their name, so if things didn't go as planned they could simply walk away. What a despicable mentality!

If you want to become a net worth millionaire investing in real estate, you will go much farther with a strong moral character and a love for your sellers rather than succumbing to this kind of myopic greed. Create a deal that works for your seller's benefit first, and also for you. If that is a subject-to deal, go for it. But don't act against their interest purely for your financial gain. In real estate and in life, *always do the right thing*.

While we are on the subject of creative financing, you should also consider the wraparound mortgage. A wraparound is where a seller who already has a mortgage on a property sells the property to you while holding back a mortgage of their own. Effectively, you're paying your mortgage to the seller and the seller continues to pay their mortgage to the bank. The same Due on Sale clause trigger may apply here, but we have still had success implementing this strategy. It works especially well when the seller wants monthly income without the hassle of renting or owning the property. You can imagine a deal where you're able to rent the house for $1500, pay him your mortgage payment of $800, and he pays his mortgage payment of $500—everyone is making money in this deal. This also works well if you bought a home, financed it, and then seller-financed it to someone else. Everyone wins!

The final way we'll talk about for funding real estate is the old-fashioned way—working hard, earning money, and paying cash. Granted, if you want to invest $100,000 in real estate, it may take you a long time to save up that kind of money. But that shouldn't stop you from getting involved in real estate investing. You can begin marketing, negotiating with sellers, getting contracts on properties, and then wholesaling those properties by selling the contracts to other investors. If you wholesale twenty properties over the course of a year and average $7,500 on each wholesale, after taxes you have probably made about $100,000! Imagine what you could do then.

You could buy a $100,000 investment property and own it free and clear, creating amazing cash flow. You could buy five investment properties, putting $20,000 down on each and financing the rest commercially. You could use those cash reserves as your own line of credit, being your own bank, borrowing from that balance to BRRRR properties over and over again.

No matter which method you choose to focus on as your primary mechanism, you should have an understanding of all of these methods and more that we haven't addressed. Think of them as tools in your belt. Sometimes you need a hammer, but sometimes you need a screwdriver. One method of funding won't work for every deal, so don't pigeon-hole yourself. We can't help but think of the people we know who have only ever bought with seller financing because of their aversion to banks. How many deals have they passed on that could have made them money if only they were willing to put the debt in their own name? Learn how to use all of the tools and put them in your belt. You will be on your way to becoming a net worth millionaire real estate investor in no time!

Notes

"This is the way."

~The Mandalorian

CHAPTER 5: THE WAY

"Every person who invests in well-selected real estate in a growing section of a prosperous community adopts the surest and safest method of becoming independent, for real estate is the basis of wealth." - Theodore Roosevelt

President Roosevelt's sentiments seldom have rung truer than in the uncertainty of the present times. However, despite the self-evident importance of a career in real estate investing, it is hardly ever a straightforward journey. If only there was a one-size-fits-all strategy to real estate! Take it for what it's worth, but there is no single, easy way through. Try as we may, we simply cannot give you a one-page guide or flow chart on how to become a net worth millionaire real estate investor. Don't despair, though. We can still teach you.

Your journey will not look exactly like ours, though. There is no cut-and-paste where "if you do what they did you'll get what they got." Your strengths and weaknesses are dissimilar to everyone else's and the opportunities and threats you experience will vary wildly compared to others'. While we can assure you that you *can* become a net worth millionaire through real estate investing, the *way* you do that will be unique to your own set of circumstances, those you're in and those you'll help create.

> **Key Point:** There is no cut-and-paste way to simply replicate the success of other real estate investors. Everyone is different and everyone's path is different. Spend time learning what has worked for others and find what works best for you.

Once you have accepted that your real estate journey will be uniquely your own and can get yourself out of the habit of template thinking, you are truly ready to learn. We can teach you a number of strategies to employ on your real estate journey, each with its own merit and a place in your arsenal. As you deploy the tools at your disposal, your investor-self will begin to emerge. What we mean by that is that only by using a mixture of the techniques you are about to learn here will you truly know what works best for you.

You may see yourself as someone who wants to pick one thing and do it extremely well. Or you may find that you're someone who values deploying a diversified and well-rounded investment strategy to achieve your goals. Whatever decisions you make as you start working toward your dreams should be educated decisions. Here we'll try to educate you on wholesaling, flipping, renting, and so forth, but we want you to look at this as an academic exercise. We want you to learn these ways to invest, choosing later which to apply to your specific set of circumstances.

Wholesaling

The word wholesaling has a different meaning in the real-estate context compared to its retail counterpart. In its more familiar context, wholesaling occurs when somebody sells goods in bulk, charging a lower price and banking on the volume of the sales to someone else (usually a retailer) who then repackages and distributes the goods further at a higher price. However, in the real estate context, wholesaling doesn't involve selling a lot of properties at bargain prices at one time. Far from it! In this context, a wholesaler first establishes a contract with a homeowner interested in selling his or her property. Then, the wholesaler finds someone else, usually an established real estate investor, interested in buying that home at a higher price.

The wholesaler's profits, in this situation, come from the buyer alone, amounting to the spread between the end buyer's agreed purchase price and the wholesaler's original contract price. If you enter an assignable contract with a seller for $90,000 and assign it to an end buyer at $100,000, the assignment fee of $10,000 is the wholesaler's profit for finding the deal, securing it by contract, marketing it to end-buyers, and arranging it for closing.

For the typical wholesaler, no money actually changes hands until they have found a buyer/assignee and that end-buyer actually closes on the deal. You don't have any money out of pocket except perhaps earnest money to secure the deal and any inspection costs you incur in doing your due diligence to represent the property accurately to prospective buyers. However, it is important to know that if you are unsuccessful at finding an assignee, you remain under contract and your seller expects you to close on the property. It is for this reason that many wholesalers include contingency clauses that give the freedom to back out of the contract.

As a matter of principle, always be honest with your sellers. If you are locking up a property with the intention of wholesaling it, do not mislead your seller by saying that you are surely going to close on it. Remember, *always do the right thing*. Tell the seller that you work with a pool of investors and you are going to shop the contract to them, but if you are unsuccessful you may have to back out. Never string a seller along and then pull the rug out from under them at the last minute! If you have other peoples' interests at heart, you'll go far in this business.

> **Key Point:** If you have other peoples' interests at heart, you'll go far in this business.

Many would-be real estate investors get their start in wholesaling, for a variety of reasons, and you may wish to do so too. Perhaps you do not have the capital or borrowing capacity to fund deals yet but know a lot of people and have the social graces to generate motivated seller leads, negotiate contracts, and find other investors who will capitalize on the opportunities presented. Some wholesalers start out without all the pieces of the puzzle but find them along the way. This allows them to capitalize on the opportunities that come their way, flipping the houses they get under contract or buying them to hold rentals in their own portfolio. Some simply lack the long-term vision necessary to build a rental portfolio, valuing the instant cash income received through wholesaling more than the commitment required to successfully maintain a rental portfolio. There is substantially less risk in wholesaling and the income is created much more quickly, so it is easy to fall in love with it.

If you are looking to get into wholesaling, you could look at it a few different ways. (1) Wholesaling may be a small steppingstone in the process which gets you into other areas of real estate investing. (2) Wholesaling could become and remain one part of a holistic approach toward your real estate investing. (3) Wholesaling could become a lucrative and self-sustaining business you operate concurrently with your real estate investing aspirations. Let us examine each of these views of wholesaling on its own merits.

First off, let us look at what you can expect by viewing wholesaling as a steppingstone. Assuming your goal is to get into flipping real estate, buying and holding rentals, building, developing, or some other strategy that requires a substantial amount of funds later on, wholesaling could be a quick fix for getting the capital that you need to get that ball rolling. If you only have a few thousand to begin with, consider spending it on lead generation (marketing) or pick any number of creative strategies to generate those leads. You should factor in a mixture of cold calling, direct mail, social media ads, and pay-per-click ads in your sales efforts. Once you get those leads, if you can convert them to binding contracts, you will be able to sell your interest in those contracts to another investor who has the capacity to close on it. One major upside to this is that you will have very little of your own cash in the deal. Budget for your marketing dollars, earnest money, and any inspection costs you may front to make sure the deal is marketable to an end-buyer. When you assign that to a buyer and it closes, they come over and stand in your shoes and you make the agreed upon assignment fee. Everyone wins.

Wholesaling is a great first step, as it helps you with what we call "forced learning." It forces you to learn processes that you must refine and perfect over the course of your investing to get ahead and realize your dreams. For instance, learning lead generation, communicating and negotiating with a seller, quickly and reliably analyzing renovation needs of a home, securing an end buyer/assignee, and learning contract legalese are just some of the things you'll need to master along the way. The beauty of this process is in the fact that even when you fail, you're learning! And that education is not as expensive as the education you get when you buy a flip house that fails miserably. Plus, when your wholesaling goes well, you may make a few thousand, or even tens of thousands, to put toward the next step of your journey toward The First Million!

This brings us to the second way you could view wholesaling—the holistic approach. As you become proficient in wholesaling, you will realize that you may be able to make much more on these deals by buying them yourself rather than assigning them. Perhaps you are now your own lead generation source for your flipping and rental business. What then? Do you stop wholesaling altogether? The reality is different for everybody, but some investors do just that because they want to focus their business interests into one or a few other areas of real estate investing, believing the time spent wholesaling could be better spent in other ways. A holistic approach, however, may prove that keeping wholesaling as part of your repertoire is exactly what your operation needs. Assuming your lead generation practices are producing viable leads, it would be silly to forego the opportunity to capitalize on those leads when the opportunity presents itself. We recommend keeping wholesaling in your bag of tricks, regardless of where your priorities lie. This will come in handy when you get a deal on a house that doesn't fit your investing model. Keeping your wholesaling chops fresh will allow you to turn even that deal into cash. This cash can then fund another acquisition or get pumped back into your marketing budget.

> **Key Point:** Money made in wholesaling can be pumped right back into marketing!

Thirdly, we want you to think of wholesaling as running a business. Many people began with wholesaling as a first step, thinking they'll either move on to other areas of investing or that it would remain part of a holistic approach. However, they quickly realize that they can operate with very little capital invested and produce steady, scalable income. With successful lead generation, effective negotiation skills, and strong networking, you can build a business around wholesaling that creates a fantastic stream of revenue. Assume you send 1000 mailers, get 3 viable leads, close 1, and make $10,000 assigning it to a buyer. What would happen if you sent out 2,000 mailers? 10,000 mailers? 100,000 mailers? We are talking about serious growth potential!

It may very well turn out that you become proficient at running a business, managing people, and converting opportunity into revenue. Perhaps you already are. Successful wholesaling business owners learn early on that they have the capacity to grow their small efforts into large systems with widespread impact. Instead of closing one wholesale every month or two and spending that money on a vacation, they pumped the profits back into the machine to keep it growing at the most impressive (yet sustainable) rate that they could. We have seen companies grow from infancy to closing 200 deals a year in less than four years. With gross revenue of over two million a year, you may just decide to forego other kinds of real estate investing and focus on wholesaling exclusively. Even if you don't, we ask that you give it your best and treat it with all the seriousness and singularity of purpose that you can muster.

While running a seven-figure wholesaling business may not sound like your thing, it probably wasn't what many real estate investors set out to do before you. Dreaming and visualizing are as important as planning and executing. Just keep your options open and your goals lofty. Wholesaling really can be lucrative, whether it is your full-time gig or a steppingstone on the way to your other real estate endeavors.

Flipping
Flipping looks easy. You've seen it done on television. Maybe you've seen us do it. If you allow yourself to believe it, the consistent messaging that pop culture seems to blast about flipping is that it is easy, fun, and extremely profitable. Well, it isn't exactly as advertised. We are here to tell you that TV is fake and flipping is extremely hard. It is exceptionally difficult, fraught with peril, and could easily lead you straight into financial disaster. However, you should definitely be flipping houses!

When we began our journey, we originally planned to acquire a small portfolio of rentals to provide nominal cash flow and a decent return on our investment, planning for retirement many years away. We had no intention of flipping and certainly didn't want to wholesale. Now, we are flipping like crazy! But there is a lot you need to know before you start thinking it looks in reality like it does on TV. It simply doesn't.

> **Key Point:** TV is fake, and flipping is hard. Don't go into this thinking it will be smooth sailing. It is fraught with peril.

One of the most obvious ways people misunderstand flipping is in the number-crunching. It seems like simple math, doesn't it? The house costs $100,000 to buy. It needs $50,000 worth of work on it, and it will sell for $200,000. Estimated profit: an easy $50,000! We hate to say it, but that's TV math right there. You may receive a rude awakening if you base your decisions on TV math, but we are here to clear it up for you. Though flipping houses, in the real world, is not as profitable as they make it appear on TV, it can still make you really good money. It's why wholesaling works so well too, because someone else sees the value in flipping the house that you wholesale to them. Let us take a closer look.

Say you come across a house in disrepair that costs $100,000 to buy. First off, you should add to that the cost of borrowing or deploying that money, say 3% (if you put it on an interest only construction loan at your local bank), which comes out to $3,000. If it is a three-month renovation and it takes another three months to sell, add your holding costs to the running total of expenses, perhaps $6,000. You estimated $50,000 in repairs at first glance, but you didn't have x-ray vision to see behind the drywall. There will always, and we mean always, be something that your contractor finds that you didn't plan ahead for. Maybe that adds 10% or $5,000 to the total renovation. When you sell it, don't forget that you have to pay realtors, traditionally 6% between the two of them. Depending on where you live, you may pay about 1-5% in closing costs and perhaps even some of the buyers' requested repairs. So, take about 10% off the sale price to get your net, before subtracting your expenses. This is how it looks:

End Sale Price:	$200,000
Closing Costs, Repairs, Realtor Fees:	-$20,000
Renovation Costs:	-$55,000
Holding Costs:	-$6,000
Acquisition Cost:	-$103,000
Gross Profits:	$16,000

Looking at these numbers, the optimist in you may be tempted to think, "Well, that's still $16,000 profit! That's pretty good. If I put 15% down on the construction loan, I made more than a 100% return on my investment in six months." You'd be right. But don't forget that the IRS will tax that income at the highest rate possible because it qualifies as short-term capital gains. And if you tithe or otherwise give charitably as you prosper, which we highly encourage you to do, your net earnings may actually only amount to eight or nine grand!

Once you know where to get all the numbers, you can make more realistic estimates and tailor your expectations accordingly. This will be absolutely pivotal to developing a well-rounded growth plan for your real estate investment business. Ditch the TV math and know that Murphy's Law will always apply in flipping.

Now, having said all of that, still—you should definitely be flipping. You just need to know the numbers before you get into it. You can't assume that a $100k acquisition that will sell for $200k will make you a mint. The juice is not always worth the squeeze. But you can make real money. In the example above, even a small change in parameters would result in different numbers. For instance, if that same house only took $25,000 and one month to get it ready to sell, your net profits would be substantially higher. If the market climbed and you sold it for $220,000, your spread just went up significantly.

To be able to flip effectively and profitably, you need to look at flipping like a business. Better yet, learn to appreciate that each house flip is itself a business, with its own profit-and-loss statement. Work backward with the end goal in mind: the sale of the house at a set price. Deduct the expenses associated with the project and a desired, built-in profit margin that makes the project worthwhile. In your analysis of every deal, build in a desired threshold of what gross profit would make it worthwhile to you. Doing the math above, you can then arrive at the price you are willing to pay for the home. If your seller or wholesaler is willing to accept that price or less, you're in business. If not, move on to the next one. It's a math problem. You cannot get emotionally attached to a flipping project. Repeat after me: it's a business.

Once you can view each house flip as a business, you'll realize that flipping can generate income to help you reach your goals in a few different ways. Much like wholesaling, it could be that you flip a few houses on your way toward your other real estate investment goals, simply because it provides capital that you can throw at something else. It may become and remain part of your holistic approach to real estate investing, being another valuable asset in your toolkit that you pull out when certain deals come across your desk. Or, you guessed it, you may accidentally start a flipping business that is profitable and scalable!

> **Key Point:** Consider each flip house as a standalone business with its own profit-and-loss sheet.

We know investors who originally intended to build a fairly simple rental portfolio and used flipping to generate capital to get them there. However, it became apparent that they were especially good at flipping houses, so much so that they continuously increased their bandwidth to do more and more of it. Instead of keeping homes as rentals, which would make good money over a long period of time, they grew to where they were flipping and selling everything they could get their hands on. Growing to that volume allowed them to minimize expenses and accept smaller margins. This, then, allowed them to offer to pay more for houses than their competition, creating an even larger volume of deal flow. Now, their flipping business generates far more income than the rental portfolio would have.

This is a convenient template that you could follow as you start on this journey, then refine over time with the lessons you pick up along the way. Speaking from our own experience, we view flipping as more than a steppingstone. In fact, to us it is just one component of the whole. When a lead comes across the desk, we first analyze it with the end goal in mind that we are trying to build a strong and profitable rental portfolio.

Afterward, we examine its potential if we were to flip it. We have found that, often, a deal works marginally as a rental but may work better as a flip—as in, we could make a little money over a long period of time as a rental, but we could make a mint right now if we flip it. We urge you to do the same. Weigh the short-term gains versus the long-term ones. For instance:

- We weigh in the balance whether or not we've got the bandwidth to add another flip to our current active projects.
- We consider how hard I'm working our Project Manager right now on our existing projects.
- We consider opportunity cost, because if we take on this project it may mean the next deal has to go by the wayside.

If the analysis makes us want to flip it, we are often quite glad we've got the capacity to do so. Cashing big checks is a lot of fun. By the way, if it doesn't look like a rental we'd keep or a flip we want to mess with, we always consider the wholesale. You've simply got to be well-rounded. To us, the only way to become a net worth millionaire is by being able to make an educated decision on how to handle the deals that come your way and work diligently to find the way to make them profitable.

Rentals

In our opinion, wholesaling and flipping are ways to generate income, while rentals are the key to generating wealth. Wholesaling and flipping are sources of active income, which means that you have to constantly monitor the progress on these sorts of projects and provide tender loving care as they develop, while a rental portfolio can be maintained almost entirely passively. Active and passive income sources each have their place, and both should be created along the way.

"Active income" is income that stops if you stopped putting in the work to produce it. Your traditional day job is active income, trading time for money. If you begin wholesaling or flipping to generate revenue, you may be able to create a fantastic annual income. However, unless you have built a business around wholesaling or flipping, systematizing well and hiring all the right people, it will perpetually require substantial focus on your part to remain operating at that level. Even if you create a well-designed business that runs like a machine, you will still need to keep an eye on things, connect with your workers, and make sure that the business is being run in accordance with your moral values in your absence. You'll have to stay active to some degree to ensure your business prospers.

If your goal is to obtain financial freedom through the creation of passive income, rental real estate is an efficient and scalable way to achieve what you what. We won't try too hard to sell you on this as the way because if you're reading this book you are likely already sold on the idea and you want to learn how. There are countless ways to grow a portfolio of rentals that will produce your desired cash flow, but before we get into it, let us get some leg work out of the way.

> **Key Point:** If you aim to become a net worth millionaire real estate investor, acquiring a rental portfolio will get you there much faster than you think!

First off, you need to determine what your goals are in terms of creating passive income. It would be easy to simply say "I want 10 single family rentals" or "I want 150 doors." But that doesn't mean anything in terms of income. You could overpay for each of those doors, creating negative equity and actually acquiring liabilities rather than assets. You need to be able to articulate that you want a certain dollar amount each month in passive cash flow, whether that number is $500 or $50,000 per month.

Then, if you want to dial in on what that number really needs to be, back up and take a look at your spending. When we encourage people to go through this exercise, most have no idea what they need in order to retire comfortably. We recommend carving out a few hours to analyze your historical household spending, much like you did if you followed our advice in the Debt chapter. If you know exactly how much you're spending on a monthly basis, you know what it takes to live the lifestyle you are currently living. Your historical spending analysis won't lie.

Once you have your analysis and, hopefully, your budget completed, you should then know how much money you would need to create in passive income to replace your current income. If you historically spent $5,000 per month, then perhaps you only need $5,000 monthly in passive income to be so-called financially free. With that amount of passive income, you could quit your active income producing work and let the passive income pay for your lifestyle. But what if you want to improve your lifestyle beyond that? Dream bigger and make that number $10,000 monthly. Already financially well off and want to go bigger? The sky is the limit. Shoot for $50,000 per month or even $250,000 if you feel up to the challenge! That's the thing about your dreams; they're yours.

Since the purpose of this book is to teach you how to make your first million in rental real estate, let's assume, somewhat conservatively, you simply want to replace your $60,000 salary job with $5,000 per month in cash flow. So, how can you create that much in passive income? The options available to you are many, for instance:

- You could have 50 houses that bring in a cash flow of $100 monthly after expenses.
- Or, you could have 25 houses that generate $200 monthly after expenses.
- You could have 10 houses that bring in $500 per month after expenses.
- You could have 5 houses that establish a cash flow of $1,000 per month after expenses.
- Lastly, you could have 1 house that generates $5,000 monthly after expenses.

To decide what route to take, you need to know your level of risk tolerance and debt aversion, two very different but related topics of discussion.

Risk tolerance is how much risk you are willing to take in a given investment or investment strategy. In a sense, it describes how easily you can sleep at night knowing the risks involved in how you are playing the game. Some people are very risk tolerant, willing to throw caution to the wind, swing for the fences, and bet it all on black. On the other hand, some are not willing to risk their hard-earned money and cannot stand the thought of losing it in their efforts to earn more.

Debt aversion, similar to risk tolerance, is a person's ability to sleep at night knowing they owe money to someone else. People who are debt averse want to buy in cash or pay down their debts quickly, being free from owing anyone anything.

Those who have little or no debt aversion do not get emotional about owing money, often being carefree in borrowing to grow their real estate portfolio.

As you could imagine, there is a balancing point for each person on the scale of risk tolerance, and your safe place may be close to the middle—not so risk tolerant that you'd risk losing it all on one deal but not so intolerant that you're afraid to play the game. Debt aversion has a balancing point for most people as well—not so debt averse that you refuse to play the game with other people's money but not so free with borrowing that you go broke on the way to bankrupt.

To simplify how risk tolerance and debt aversion apply in our investment strategies, let's analyze two scenarios.

Scenario 1: You could generate $5,000 monthly in passive income by owning 50 houses that each bring in a cash flow $100 per month after all expenses and debt services have been cleared on each one.

Scenario 2: You could generate $5,000 monthly in passive income by owning 10 houses, free and clear that cash flow $500 per month after all expenses.

In Scenario 1, you carry a lot of debt, but the income is currently more than enough to cover the debt, such that it still creates the cash flow to meet your passive income needs. Those who are less risk tolerant or more debt averse see greater value in Scenario 2, where there are fewer roofs and HVACs to go bad, conceivably fewer tenant issues, and no loans are held on the properties, making the cash flow higher for each of the rental properties.

Those who have higher risk tolerance may value having a larger portfolio, where each additional home poses its own set of risks but add considerable depth and variety to the diversified whole of the portfolio. If you have ten homes and one is vacant, you have a 90% occupancy rate. If you have fifty homes with one vacancy, you have 98% occupancy. The same analysis can be made with roofs, HVACs, and house fires. The more doors you have, the less each individual property affects the entire portfolio.

Some choose to buy a rental home, work to pay it off in full, then buy another, and so on. This strategy is certainly valid and is a slower, less risky, debt averse way of reaching your goal. Others who are less debt averse may be willing to use other people's money more freely, scaling the portfolio very quickly, despite the increased debt and risk involved. There are pros and cons to both strategies, you simply need to determine where you fit on the spectrum to decide which strategy works best for you.

We can openly tell you that we are middle-of-the-road in risk tolerance, as we are not willing to bet it all on one house, but we are certainly willing to jump in the game when we think we spot a good deal. Regarding debt aversion—we hate consumer debt. But in the context of real estate investing, there is no faster way to become a net worth millionaire in real estate than by using other people's money. To be absurdly clear, we love the debt that we have on our portfolio, but we keep it in balance, never exceeding 75% leveraged on any one piece of property. More on that later.

So, you can make an educated decision on which direction to go. Choosing between Scenario 1 and Scenario 2, let's examine how these play out over time and see what happens. Let's pretend that each house is worth $100,000 and, because you are a sharp negotiator, or lucky, or both, you are able to acquire them with an investment of $75,000 (ignoring the breakdown of acquisition, closing, holding, and renovation costs, for simplicity). Assume each home rents for $900, for a round starting number.

In Scenario 2, you save up $15,000 to put 20% down on the first house, with a debt of $60,000 at 5% interest amortized over 20 years. The monthly payment is just under $400. The $900 rent is reduced by 10% paid to the management company (-$90), another 15% eaten up by repairs, maintenance, vacancy, and anticipated capital expenditures, or CapX (-$135), your property taxes we will assume to be -$90 monthly, and insurance we will assume to be -$75 per month. In this Scenario, your cash flow is $110 per month. Adding this cash flow to the principal every month would pay the house off in approximately fourteen years! To really pay the home off quickly, you would need to add substantial principal payments to each monthly payment. Adding another $1000 monthly, from your other sources of income, to the payment, it pays it off in approximately four years. Presumably, then, the debt averse investor will buy his or her second property—after saving up another sizable down payment, that is.

In Scenario 1, let us see what happens if we approach the strategy a bit differently. Someone who is not debt averse may be willing to attack from a few other angles. Perhaps you're willing to put 10% down ($7500) and amortize it over 25 years. Would you believe the payment is near enough the same, just under $400 per month? If you had $15,000 saved up, that means you can do two of these deals at the same time! Now your cash flow is twice as much, since you're using other people's money as leverage. Instead of $110 monthly cash flow on one house, you're making $220 per month in cash flow on two houses. However, to get house number three you've got to save up another down payment. This happens at a much faster rate than Scenario 2 but can still be challenging because cash/capital is often limited and you may not be able to come up with more down payments in a short amount of time.

What if you could buy a house without deploying any capital at all, though? Well, there are a handful of ways to do that, which we've already discussed: You could buy with owner/seller financing, where the seller carries the note and maybe you are able to put zero down. You could buy the house subject to the existing mortgage, leaving the debt in the seller's name. You could buy the property on a land contract or contract for deed, where you can obtain an equitable interest in the property without having to deploy much capital or even financing with a traditional bank.

We won't go over each of these strategies again, but one beautiful method worth revisiting, however, is the BRRRR strategy. Remember, this is where you buy the property outright, often in cash or with an existing line of credit, then renovate as necessary, rent it out, refinance your cash back out of the property, perhaps paying off the line of credit you used, and repeat the process. Assuming you had $75,000 in cash, you could buy the property outright. Scenario 2 people would think "woohoo, our first rental home owned free and clear!" That $900 monthly rent is still reduced by 10% property management, approximately 15% for vacancy, maintenance, repairs, and CapX, $90 for taxes, and $75 for insurance. This results in a cash flow of $510 per month, by that math. Setting that aside each month, it would still take you more than 12 years to save up another $75,000. So that's not what you do if you are in Scenario 1. Rather, you find a bank that will refinance the home at 75% loan-to-value (LTV) and pull all of your cash out!

Some banks will only finance a percentage of the purchase price, wanting the borrower to have some skin in the game. They may only lend 75%-90% of the *purchase price*. We like it when banks lend 75%-80% of the *value* (LTV) because you can pull out most, all, or even more than the $75,000 and deploy it all over again on the next house!

It gets really fun when you can use a line of credit for the initial acquisition. If a bank will extend to you a line of credit, whether unsecured or secured by some asset, you can use that line of credit for the acquisition, then refinance the asset to pay the line of credit back down to a zero balance. Rinse and repeat over and over again until you reach your goal for passive income. Sometimes the journey is as beautiful as the destination!

Scenario 2 is considered the safer, but slower, path to financial freedom. If you are diligent enough to pay down principal or save to buy in cash, you can build a small portfolio of rentals that will meet the passive income goal you have set for yourself. Scenario 1 appears riskier and scares the debt averse, but it is a much faster way to build wealth and allow you to reach your goals. One thing to realize is the return on investment (ROI) is significantly higher in Scenario 1 due to the number of ways rental real estate makes you money.

There are four primary ways that rental real estate can make you money:
- Cash flow
- Appreciation
- Depreciation and other tax advantages
- Principal reduction

When the tenant pays $900 in rent on a home owned free and clear, it may generate a cash flow of $510 per month, as we've seen above. This amounts to $6,120 annually. That $100,000 home may appreciate at a rate of 3%, on average, so in the first year, it grows by an unrealized amount of $3,000. The home is depreciated on taxes, so taxes paid on the income is appropriately reduced, though it is unlikely to reduce it zero. But, since there is no debt, there is no mortgage interest deduction or, for that matter, principal reduction benefit.

On a leveraged home that only cash flows $110 monthly, or $1,320 annually, it appears that the return is far less significant. However, the $3000 in unrealized appreciation remains the same, whether there is debt on the property or not. The home depreciates the same, plus there are additional deductions, such as the mortgage interest deduction, potentially sufficient to offset all of the income of the property and create a passive loss that carries forward to future years. And, since there is debt on the property that is paid down every month, an amortization calculator would quickly tell us that in the first year, the principal was reduced by about $308 monthly, or $3,700 for the year. Arguably, the total return in this scenario is as good as or better than the former.

The most beautiful thing about this analysis is the calculation of the return on investment (ROI). In Scenario 2, assume the annual benefit in cash flow, appreciation, and tax advantages make for a $10,000 increase in your net worth. On a $75,000 investment, your ROI is 13.33% (represented by X in the formula):

10,000 / 75,000 = X / 100
X = (2/15) * 100
X = 13.33%

In Scenario 1, assume the annual benefit in cash flow, appreciation, tax advantages, and principal reduction to make for a $10,000 increase in your net worth. If you put twenty percent down on the purchase, $15,000, your ROI is an astonishing 66.66%! If you deployed the full $75,000 in increments of $15,000 each on five identical deals, your ROI remains at 66.66% but your annual increase in net worth is now $50,000!

Take it a step further and assume you refinanced all but $5,000 out of the deal. In fairness, maybe your net worth increase is only $9000, since the cash flow is lower here. The ROI is an almost unbelievable 180% on your money.

But wait, there's more. What if you could pull out all of your cash on that $75,000 deal? Now the cash flow is lower but the appreciation, tax advantages, and principal reduction are still very much present. Perhaps the annual increase in your net worth is only $7,500 on this one house. With zero down, what is your ROI? Infinite! Go ahead. Try to plug those numbers into your calculator and watch it cry with delight.

What does this mean though? Well, if you give me zero dollars and I give you back a $100, how many times would you do it? Once? Twice? A hundred times? A thousand times? If you could become a net worth millionaire using other people's money, creating a near infinite rate of return and have enough passive income to meet your goals, would you do it? The answer should be *absolutely*!

But let's recall risk tolerance and debt aversion for a moment. Some investors want no debt while others can still sleep at night knowing they owe banks almost as much as a property is worth. For us, the balance is being risk tolerant enough to get in the game and play hard yet debt averse enough to maintain no more than a 60-70% loan to value across our entire portfolio at any one point in time. With that mindset, even if the market took a dive and you were forced to liquidate some of your assets, you're still in a strong position.

You will probably not become a net worth millionaire if you only buy one rental property, though. Or at least you won't get there very quickly. You can get there in Scenario 2, it will just take a lot longer, especially if you are not already a high-income earner throwing significantly more principal against the debt or buying in all cash. If you attempt Scenario 1, you can certainly get there more quickly, as your annual increase in net worth grows with each home you acquire and does so automatically. With the equity spread in our hypothetical deal structure, you will become a net worth millionaire long before you hit your passive income goal!

Other Ways

There are a number of other ways in real estate you could choose to become a net worth millionaire that we have not discussed, each with their own set of pros and cons. For instance:

- You could build new construction single family homes to sell or rent.
- You could build multifamily apartments, whether duplexes, triplexes, quadruplexes, or larger, to sell or rent.
- You could buy raw land in anticipation of appreciation or to develop and subdivide.
- You could create systems and practices for lead generation and sell those leads to others pursuing their goals in real estate.
- You could work hard at your day job to build wealth that you then lend to others investing in real estate.
- You could become a hard money lender, invest your money in real estate investment trusts, or put your money in large syndicated multifamily deals.
- You could syndicate other investors into your own large multifamily deals.
- You could even build businesses around these and countless other aspects of real estate.

How you choose to become a net worth millionaire in real estate is up to you. What we want to teach you is that you are not restricted to one strategy. Diversify your efforts and create multiple streams of revenue. If you follow our lead, you'll wholesale, flip, and build a rental portfolio in addition to your day job or other business you may run. The first million will come a lot easier than you think.

THE FIRST MILLION

Notes

A little learning is a dangerous thing;
Drink deep, or taste not the Pierian spring:
There shallow draughts intoxicate the brain,
And drinking largely sobers us again.

~ **Alexander Pope**

CHAPTER 6: THE KNOW

"Knowledge is power," as they say, and countless life experiences of your own have confirmed this saying. Real Estate investing, as broad and exciting as this field is, is really a rabbit hole of learning. The further you want to go, the further you will see it is possible to go. The more you learn, the more you realize how much you don't know. I love learning and it seems as if every step of the way we are learning from our experiences, experiences of others, and opportunities missed. At this point in your journey, the key is to rapidly accelerate your learning so that you can avoid the pitfalls and mistakes that could cost you big.

It is easy to simply search the internet for how to learn about investing in real estate and become inundated with opportunities for education. There is a new guru popping up every day and countless people will take your money on the promise to teach you how to get rich quickly. There are innumerable scams for all the suckers out there willing to click the clickbait and punch in their credit card information. Be careful.

> **Key Point:** At this point in the journey, the key is to rapidly accelerate your learning so that you can avoid the pitfalls and mistakes that could cost you big.

If you are dead set on taking some form of course in real estate investing, you are spoiled for choice. However, we advise you to think very carefully before signing up to any course or mentorship of a self-proclaimed expert or guru. Take the time to look at the reviews of people who have been enrolled on the course; many of these are an honest review of people's experience with the course. Try to get genuine feedback from someone else who has taken the course themselves and converted that education into practice.

We think that it's also important to look at the actual experience of the teacher and their motivation for transmitting that knowledge. There are tons of internet-famous investors who have made a name for themselves on social media and offer to teach you the tips and tricks to becoming a millionaire real estate investor. However, some of these have only a modest amount of experience and are teaching because it is an easier way to make money. Just because someone has created a likable internet personality and appears to have reached a desirable level of success does not mean they are suitable to follow. Social media is full of people projecting what they want you to see because it sells, not the reality behind the curtain.

Regardless, we propose that you overwhelm yourself with educational opportunities and experiences. Listen to every podcast you can find on real estate. Watch every YouTube video. Read every book. Take it all with a grain of salt but take it all in. Study the game like you are back in school, where knowledge of the material will be on the test—because a lot of it will. When you begin to understand real estate investing, keep studying. Then, when you get in the game, keep studying.

Those of you with very little knowledge of the field may feel overwhelmed when you hear or read terms that are unfamiliar, but these gaps in knowledge can begin to be filled in by participating in some of the following:

- Seminars: Free seminars give you some insight into real estate, but it usually involves a sales pitch trying to persuade you buy one of their programs. A paid program, however, gives you a more personalized experience and an opportunity to dive deeper into real estate. Don't let your location limit you; travel if you need to. Just be careful, as we've said.

- Group meetings: These meetings are cheap or even free in some cases. Generally, it is a great opportunity to network with individuals who are far more experienced in the field than you. Use the best of your communication skills to mingle with investors who can give you tips and tricks to succeed in real estate. Soak it all in and don't be afraid to ask an experienced investor to coffee or lunch sometime.

- Books: This is still one of the best means of gathering valuable information. There are tons of books that are available to purchase online that draw from people's practical experience in the real estate world. More than ever, e-books and audiobooks are putting knowledge at your fingertips and right in your ears.

- Podcasts: If you're not really the type of person to sit down and read, listening to someone speak about different areas of real estate may be the next best thing, or even better, for you. There are countless real estate podcasts, so find the ones that feature experienced and generous hosts and guests, providing real value to your education.

- Forums and Social Media Groups: These are great for answering questions that you have about real estate; you can also look at others' questions and answers so that you can gain further knowledge.

- Blogs: Blogs have been around for a while and cover a vast number of topics. Passionate blog writers aim to share both simple and more detailed information to help you get the ball rolling.

Gaining knowledge is an important step that you will take when getting insight into any subject. However, implementing what you have learned is just as important. You should try and use the resources that you've found and knowledge you've gained to try things out for yourself. Everyone's learning experience is different, so pick the method that works best for you or use some or all of them. Then, as quickly as you can, put that knowledge to work.

Quite possibly, the best educator is experience. Get in the game. Many people learn by doing, as it forces you to learn along the way. No successful real estate investor knew it all before they got started. Rather, you should know enough to get started and then learn more and more every step of the way. Experience teaches you what not to do. Experience teaches you what you can do better. Experience teaches you lessons that will stick with you much longer than those you read in a book or heard in a podcast. Once you start investing, the learning truly begins. Once the learning begins, it doesn't stop.

THE FIRST MILLION

Notes

"Deals work best when each side gets something it wants from the other."

~ Donald J. Trump,

Trump: The Art of the Deal

CHAPTER 7: THE DEAL

Finally, we get to talk about the hardest part in real estate investing—finding the deal! Where most people think the hardest part is finding the money to fund the deal or gaining the education necessary to tackle the deal, the hardest part is, unequivocally, finding the deal in the first place. You may have all of the real estate knowledge and tons of capital or borrowing power, but if you don't have the deal, you're not investing in real estate. Buckle up, because this chapter is going to be thick.

"I'll just get a buyer's agent and buy something off of the MLS," I hear you say, along with every other investor in your area looking for the same kind of deals you're looking to buy. "Well, I'll get creative and start networking with agents who have pocket-listings from time to time." Do that. But if you're not first on their call list, you'll probably miss all of the good ones.

"So, what do I do? How do I find and analyze the deal?" We'll help.

Finding attractive deals is the most difficult part of real estate investing because the market is so flooded with buyers in competition with one another. Competition breeds excellence, it's been said. Only the strong survive, some say. In real estate, it's *survival of the fittest* and, because of the limited supply of resources (homes/land), not everyone gets to eat. People question why we want to teach you how to make it as a real estate investor, since we are basically creating more competition for ourselves as real estate investors. But we already know that most people can't compete in this environment. If they can compete, it will only make us work harder and become better at what we do. And, the rising tide lifts all ships.

The traditional route is to just hire a buyer's real estate agent and have them find the deal for you, whether listed or otherwise. The agent has an incentive to find you investment property because they make a commission working for you. They have a greater incentive when you pay more, by the way, given that they work on a commission that is a percentage of the price. You've got to be careful how you analyze a deal brought by someone who makes more when you pay more. If you trust your agent, stick with them. We've had some stellar agents over the years and some we wouldn't trade for anything. The real key is, however, you need to know your numbers. Let me say it again—you need to know your numbers!

As an investor, you cannot rely on someone else to analyze the deal for you, whether they are your agent or otherwise. We can't tell you how many times an agent would say "this would make a great rental," but they don't have a clue how to run numbers on a cash flow analysis. The same agents may say "this would be an amazing house to flip," but they don't yet know how to run numbers to determine whether the flip would be profitable! Deal analysis falls solely on your shoulders and whether a deal is or is not a deal to you depends exclusively on the conclusions you draw. When you become proficient at running the numbers, teach your agent. If you work with wholesalers, teach them. Explain what, why, and how you want to buy, so perhaps they'll only spend time bringing you the worthwhile deals. When they bring you deals, run numbers for them so they can see why the deal does or does not work. When they work, take the deal!

Before we talk about finding the deal, you need to prepare for it by learning how best to run the numbers. Before you can properly analyze the numbers, you first need to know your goals. Are you looking to flip, to generate income for your family to live off of? Are you looking to flip in a self-directed IRA? Are you buying rentals for cash flow you need to pay your bills? Are you buying rentals as a long-term wealth building strategy with a retirement horizon of 10-20 years? How fast do you need the deal to close where you can start producing revenue? These questions, and more, will help you as you begin your deal analysis.

Let's assume for a moment that you want to flip for supplemental income and that you are currently living off of the income your day job produces. With that in mind, you'd really like to get into flipping houses on the side so you can grow your income potential to the benefit of your family and the community you support through good works. We'd like to think you have some money set aside in savings, perhaps an emergency fund and some extra cash you can use to invest. If you've already lined up either cash, private financing, or bank financing, you're ready to start looking for a deal that brings you closer to your goal.

Perhaps in your area a three bedroom, two bath house with a two-car garage and a fenced yard is an ideal flip candidate, as it is in most places. As you start looking at houses that would make for good flips, you have in mind an ideal sale price of, say, $300,000. You find a house that needs work and a sale price advertised at $200,000 and you already know it is at least priced below the After Repair Value (ARV). The first thing you do is dial in on the ARV by collecting data and, perhaps, having your favorite agent pull comparable sales (comps). There are automated valuation models (AVM) out there, used by the likes of Zillow and similar sites, that make it tempting to accept their reported value. But, an AVM is just an approximation. Don't discard it altogether, just keep AVM values as one data point within the fuller analysis. Collect other data like the tax assessment value, last sales price, and prices of other houses in the area that are for sale or recently sold. If your agent can pull real comps, you've got a lot of data from which to draw a conclusion.

Before you settle in on an ARV, though, you need to determine the level of renovation you may be giving to the property. If a good comp has been updated from the ground up and is stunning but you only plan to do paint and carpet on your flip, that may be significant to determining value. If a comp provides a good value but was not updated, perhaps you updating the flip house might bring more value. Consider also the neighborhood, amenities, school zone, crime rate, and other factors that affect value. Then, when you can confidently say "when we are done, we will list the house at __," you have your ARV.

If you are analyzing a rental, the ARV is important for you to determine equity you'll have in the home upon completion, for purposes of calculating loan-to-value and so forth. But it is far more crucial that your ARV is accurate when flipping, since your profit-and-loss hinges on whether the sale price exceeds your expenses and the cost of your investment. If you anticipate a $20,000 profit but missed the mark on the ARV by $30,000, you just lost $10,000.

Once you have the ARV for a particular house, you need to have a handle on what it will cost to get it there. For this, it's really good to have two things: a sound understanding of the cost to renovate a home and a contractor you trust. If you have one of those two things, you may be able to get by. If you have neither of those two things, you will likely lose as much sleep as you will money. Calculating repairs and updates can be tricky, but you get better with time. There are shortcuts and fill in the blank checklists you can use, but they provide guestimates at best. If you're new to the game, the best thing you can do is interview several contractors, pick from the ones you trust the most, and get multiple estimates.

Our team is really good at estimating repairs, since we have remodeled so many homes. However, one thing has been true every single time we run numbers—you're always wrong. There will always be something different about the project, so no matter what you think you'll spend, expect to spend more. Be conservative with your numbers every time. Once in a blue moon you'll land close to or better than your conservative estimate and it's a great day. However, this is one reason flipping is so hard. There will always be skeletons in the closets. If you build the cushion into your renovation budget and the deal still looks good, you're ahead of the game.

Next, you simply do the math like we did briefly in an earlier chapter. Take the ARV and subtract the cost to get it to a closing table (e.g. closing costs, commissions, requested repairs). Then subtract any holding costs you may expect (e.g. pro rata insurance, taxes, utilities, mowing, HOA fees). Next, subtract your conservative estimate of renovations and your desired profit margin. Your subtotal is the amount you are able to pay plus the cost of the money incurred to get the acquisition to a closing table. If you're using a commercial loan product, your banker may tell you that an origination fee, appraisal, closing costs, etc. would likely amount to a certain percent of the purchase price. Back that number out of the total and you have your maximum allowable offer. If you can negotiate an agreement at or below that amount, you've got a deal!

Let's put up some numbers with that formula and play this out.

ARV – Let's say	$300,000
Cost to close, say -10%,	- $30,000
Holding costs, say 6 months	- $ 6,000
Renovation	- $25,000
Desired Profit	- $20,000
Acquisition costs, ~2.5% on 200k	- $ 5,000
Maximum Allowable Offer	$214,000

As you can see, if your agent or a wholesaler brought this deal to you at $200,000, you've found a great deal and you should jump on it. If you're analyzing the deal and they want $220,000, you simply negotiate that purchase price down to where you're comfortable and then pull the trigger. If your seller won't sell at a price where you make decent money, it's not a deal and you just keep looking!

"Oh, but I love that house. It was going to look so beautiful!" Yes, maybe it would have. Perhaps you've got just the aesthetic touch or artist's eye to make it amazing. But if the numbers don't work, it does not make a good flip. Flipping a house should be run like a business. If it doesn't make money, don't do it. Don't fall in love with the house; fall in love with the numbers. If you don't love the numbers, move on to the next one.

Before we move on to deal analysis for rentals, let's consider wholesaling. One reason to run numbers on every deal you can is because even if it doesn't meet your criteria, it may meet someone else's. You may have found the deal outlined above but you don't like the neighborhood, the renovation is too much for you to handle, or you don't have the capital to take it down right now. Whatever the reason, let's assume you couldn't flip this house but the numbers clearly work. All you do to analyze the wholesale of a house is build in a wholesaler's assignment fee when you are analyzing the deal.

ARV – Let's say	$300,000
Cost to close, say -10%,	- $30,000
Holding costs, say 6 months	- $ 6,000
Renovation	- $25,000
Desired Profit for Assignee	- $20,000
Acquisition costs, ~2.5% on 200k	- $ 5,000
Assignment Fee	<u>- $ 10,000</u>
Maximum Allowable Offer	$204,000

As you can see, if you plan to wholesale the deal, now you're analyzing it for another prospective buyer/assignee to flip it with an anticipated profit of $20,000. Even then, if you contracted on the property at $204,000 and assigned it at $214,000, your assignment fee is the spread, $10,000. If you were a strong negotiator and were able to get it under contract at $194,000, you just created a bigger spread for you and the assignee. Remember, the best deals are the ones where everyone wins!

Let's talk about rentals for a bit, though. Analyze deals as wholesales and flips but also analyze them as rentals, if that is what would further your progress to your goals. Wholesaling and flipping are great ways to create income, but the key to building long term wealth is in holding the asset over time. When we speak of The First Million, the occasion on which you surpass the millionaire net worth mark and truly feel wealth is actually beginning to grow, we are really talking about what a rental portfolio can do for you almost automatically.

If part of your goal set is growing your net worth to reach that first million, you will want to keep real estate in your portfolio more often than you sell or assign it. When you flip or wholesale a house, consider your actual net worth increase. Assuming you flipped the house and made a gross profit of $50,000—not a bad day's work—what would that do to your net worth in your pursuit of the first million? Remember, the IRS is going to want their share and so you get taxed at the highest rate they can tax you. Plus, in addition to the short-term capital gains, you'll be paying self-employment tax. As mentioned before, if you are charitable (and we hope you will be) you will tithe or donate some of your gain to your local church or charities. At the end of the day as much as half of that

THE FIRST MILLION

gross profit goes away, leaving you with a net worth increase of $25,000.

I'm not saying that's a bad thing to have a cash influx of $25,000 hitting the bank account. That's a great thing. It gives you money to live on, pads your savings account, or puts capital back at your disposal for more investments. But as a net worth increase, it is a one-time shot of $25k and that's it. What if you kept the house as a rental? Let's think on that for a bit.

There are four primary ways that a rental property can make you money, remember: cash flow, principal reduction, tax advantages, and appreciation. Yes, there are others and we can't forget about the instant equity if you bought the property at a discount. But we want you to consider the difference between flipping and renting for a moment. If you buy right, you'll buy a discounted property, perhaps one that needed some work, and you'll have equity from day one—the difference between the cost of your investment and its market value. If you flip it, you're just turning some of that equity into cash, after disposition costs, taxes, tithe, etc. If you have $50k of equity in a home that you could sell for $200k, that equity would turn into about $15k cash. ($200k sale price minus ~10% disposition costs = $30k, minus taxes, tithe, etc. nets you about $15,000.) As an investment, it increased your net worth by $15,000. If you kept the house in your portfolio, that $50k equity stays on your balance sheet and increases your net worth by $50,000! Now we're cookin'!

As we talk about the four primary ways a rental can make money, we are building on top of that instant equity day after day, year after year. In a little bit, we will run a cash flow analysis. But let's assume for a moment that this home rents for $1500 and all of your expenses, to include management, debt service, and money set aside for repairs and improvements, lets you cash flow $100. That's not a lot of money, but it's another $1,200 bucks a year. And as rents go up over time, that will increase. It's nothing to write home about, but it is a positive increase to your net worth that happens automatically, day after day, year after year.

Since you have debt on the property, your monthly payment pays principal down every month. Assuming you bought a $200,000 house and your investment is $150,000, perhaps you put 10% down and your note is $135,000. Plugging terms into an amortization calculator, a 5% interest loan with a 20-year amortization tells you that you are paying the note down about $335 per month in the first year, a number that goes up over time. In year one you will have paid the note down about $4,000. Again, not a big number to write home about, but it is a positive increase to your net worth that happens automatically, day after day, year after year.

The tax advantages of rental real estate are significant. For fear of being taken too literally, we must make this disclaimer: talk to your accountant about how rental real estate would impact your specific circumstances. We will not go too deep into this, but as you educate yourself further, you'll find that the tax advantages rentals provide are the gifts that keeps on giving. That mortgage you have on the property would have deductible interest around $556 per month. The taxes, insurance, and repairs you pay for on the property are all deductible. And let's not forget about depreciation, which your CPA can help you calculate. Assume, for a moment, you have about $14,000 in deductible expenses/depreciation and your effective tax rate is

25%—you could potentially be saving $3,500 in taxes. If your accountant says you would owe that $3,500, but for your rental write-offs, your net worth just increased by another $3,500 in year one.

Lastly, appreciation is a beautiful thing. We've been told and continue to maintain that you should not buy *for* appreciation. "It's too risky and unpredictable." If you lucked out and bought in an area that gets developed or becomes the next hot spot for some reason, you could stumble upon unbelievable net worth growth by accident. If you try to buy where you think that next hot spot will be, you could get it wrong—big time. However, whatever you buy, if you buy in areas that are not obviously trending downward, you can bet that appreciation will continue to raise values over time. Even conservative estimates suggest that houses will appreciate 3-5% annually over time. That $200,000 house would conceivably be worth $210,000 after the first year if the market appreciated 5%. That's a net worth increase of $10,000 year one, just based on appreciation. And remember, it happens automatically, day after day, year after year.

That $200,000 house you could have sold for a net worth increase of $15,000, if you kept it as a rental, by the end of year one you would have increased your net worth by significantly more. You'd have the $50,000 equity already on your balance sheet. Plus, you'd have the $1,200 cash flow, another $4,000 in principal reduction, potentially $3,500 in tax savings, and another $10,000 in appreciation. At the end of year one your net worth has increased $68,700! At the end of year two, your net worth increases by about another $19,000! If your goal is to generate a little cash, sell it. If you want to grow your net worth so you can reach The First Million, keep the house! And buy several more just like it!

We need to teach you how to analyze the deal, though, so you know the property you're buying will have that positive impact on your net worth. Let's say a deal comes across your desk to buy at a discount of $100,000 with an ARV of $200,000. You find that the property needs some work and a contractor gives you an estimate of $40,000 to get it ready. Adding in a buffer for holding costs, cost of borrowing the money, and so forth, let's say you will be all-in at $150,000. You immediately know you've found a good deal because it puts $50,000 of equity on your balance sheet. But you need to know the amount for which it would rent.

You may have heard of the 1% rule as a general rule of thumb. "If a property rents for 1% of the investment, it will cash flow," one would assume. This varies from place to place, depends on your financing, and so forth. However, it provides a great starting point. If you can buy where your rents are 1% or higher, you're doing great. For us, the worse the neighborhood is, the higher that number needs to be; the better the neighborhood is, the lower that number can be. As a general rule, for us, we know that at 1% the deal will cash flow even if we are zero down, refinancing all of our cash out of the deal. If we leave a down payment in the deal, we go as low as .8% if the property is in a good area.

A more thorough analysis of the deal should be done, however, to determine the actual impact a property would have on your net worth. Let's assume that $150,000 investment was one your bank required you to put $15,000 down. Your debt is $135,000, making your equity position at $65,000.

That $135,000 debt, let's say, is on a 5% note with a 25-year amortization. Your monthly principal and interest payment is going to be $789.20. You'll want to get accurate data for taxes and insurance, as well as any other expenses. There are free investment property calculator apps and websites you can use, as well as spreadsheet tools that make calculating cash flow and return on investment easy. Find a calculator you like and plug in all of the numbers. It should look something like this, as an example:

Rents	$1,500.00
Management (-10%)	- 150.00
HOA	- 20.00
Debt	- 789.20
Taxes ($1200/yr.)	- 100.00
Insurance ($800/yr.)	- 67.00
Repairs/Maint/CapX/Vac (-15%)	- 225.00
Cash Flow	=$148.80

When calculating cash flow in your analysis of a piece of rental real estate, don't forget the cost of maintaining the property over time. It would be super easy to omit that last term (Repairs, Maintenance, CapX, and Vacancy) and say the property cash flows $373.80 per month, because that may be what actually hits the bank account. However, you will have repairs. You will have maintenance. You will have capital expenditures. You will have vacancy. There is a quantifiable multiplier that *must* be considered on the front end so that you know the deal is cash flow positive. Depending on the age of the home, likelihood of turnover, quality of management's tenant screening, etc., that multiplier may need to be higher than the 15% assumed above. Learn your market and predict based on good information.

When analyzing that deal, we could quickly conclude that it is one that we would want in our portfolio, especially if it isn't a particularly old home, is in a good school zone, and the area is more likely to appreciate than not. As a matter of fact, we'd want another hundred just like it! And you should too! Some people would analyze this deal and say the cash flow is weak, which is true, but you're not buying just for cash flow. You are buying to grow your net worth to reach The First Million. We would buy this deal all day, every day.

This is the deal that would grow your net worth over $65,000 year one and another $19,000 at the end of year two. As rents go up, appreciation compounds, and the cash flow and principal reduction keep hammering away, the impact that house has on your net worth over time would be in the hundreds of thousands. Now, imagine if you did this ten times! The First Million will come much easier and faster than you think!

But what about finding the deal? Now that you know how to analyze a deal, you need to be finding the deals to analyze. Analyze every deal that you can. If you run numbers on 100 deals, you'll be proficient enough to know a deal when you see one. You'll know at a glance, whether by using a 1% rule or one similar, that *this is the one*. You'll know this is your time to pull the trigger and add a net worth increasing rental to your portfolio. But how do you find the deal?

Key Point: Finding the deal is always the hardest part.

This is certainly the hardest part, as we've mentioned more than once. The traditional route is to get a buyer's agent and have them scour the on-market listings for what may meet your criteria. The problem is that when a deal is on market, it usually brings market price. So many people are looking at that deal because there are so many investors trying to buy rental real estate, that it is literally whoever pays the most that gets the deal, often times. That makes it exceptionally hard to get a deal at a discount on market. The problem is exacerbated by the fact that whatever price you pay, on market, generally includes the cost of commissions on both sides and perhaps closing costs. When you're feeding a seller, two agents, their brokers, and at least one title company, the price just went way up.

This is where wholesalers have an edge, to some degree. A wholesaler goes straight to motivated sellers, marketing to owners of distressed properties or prospective sellers who may need to sell quickly, avoiding the traditional listing route. If a wholesaler can put a property under contract and then assign that contract to you for a fee, there are fewer mouths to feed in the process. Conceivably, you may be able to find a better deal, especially if the wholesaler brings the deal directly to you, a motivated and ready buyer. You need to be finding those wholesalers in your market and making sure they know you're ready. If they do, they'll probably put you on their buyers list.

If you are on a wholesaler's buyers list, though, there will be numerous others with you on that list. If the wholesaler runs a strong business, they likely have a buyers list of hundreds or thousands. Then, when they get a deal under contract, they market it to everyone on their buyers list. If that reaches you, typically via email, you're looking at that deal with everyone else who is reading their email. Competition against other prospective buyers on that list means the price may be driven up, but there are still fewer mouths to feed in this scenario. You are more likely to get a better deal from a wholesaler than one on market, but that's not always the case.

What about going straight to the seller yourself? If you are driving down the street and you see a house with the gutters falling off, the grass grown up tall, and the bushes overtaking the front of the house, perhaps you should just knock on the door. Or you could write down the address, find out who owns the home by looking at the tax assessor's website, find a phone number through an online service, and give them a call. If their mailing address is to another home, write them a letter or even knock on that door. If you can get straight to the prospective motivated seller, you can often get the best deal. There are even fewer mouths to feed in the process and it is much easier to craft a deal where you and the seller both win.

Much can be said about how to find the deals, for sure. You can and should network with real estate agents in your area so they know you are looking to invest in real estate. If they know you can buy and close fast, they may think of you when they get a pocket listing that fits your criteria. If they know you will re-list the home with them when you sell, they'll have even greater incentive to bring the deal to you over someone else. Similarly, network with wholesalers. Get on buyers lists. Make sure people think of you when they get a property they are willing to assign. And network with other investors. Some investors contract on properties that they later decide to wholesale; you want them to call you. Talk about real estate. Tell people what you're trying to do. Get more people on your team that can bring you the deals.

Don't be afraid to market, either. Have you ever gotten one of the postcards in the mail that says "we buy houses" or seen the little signs on the street corner "we'll buy your house fast for cash?" Usually, these are wholesalers, but investors often market like a wholesaler trying to find properties that they can buy themselves. You can create a big list of properties you would consider buying and mail to them, whether hand written cards or postcards printed in volume. The key is getting your message in front of a sufficient number of people that you can generate real, motivated seller leads on properties that you can and would buy.

Find the deals. Analyze the deals. Buy the deals. This is how you make The First Million as a real estate investor.

THE FIRST MILLION

Notes

"No one can whistle a symphony. It takes a whole orchestra to play it."

~H.E. Luccock

CHAPTER 8: THE TEAM

In real estate, you need a team. It's as simple as that. There are some people who try to do everything themselves, but one person simply cannot do it all. In the beginning of most people's real estate journey, they look at renovating a house and they almost always have in mind what color *they* are going to paint the walls. It's easy to look at the prospect of real estate investing and think about all the things that you will be able to do, particularly because it will save you money spent paying someone else to do it. However, because of the numerous steps within the process, it would be beneficial to get this out of the way early—you simply cannot do this alone.

Even if you think you can do it alone, what you'll find is that you spend more money trying to save money than you would have spent if you had just delegated properly. More than that, still, is the *opportunity cost* of trying to do too much yourself. While you may be able to save $25/hour doing something yourself, not having to pay someone else to do it, you may be costing yourself thousands of dollars in missed opportunities where your time could have been better spent. But "if you want it done right, you'll do it yourself," I hear you say. I'm sorry, but that is just not always true.

> **Key Point:** Know the opportunity cost of trying to do something yourself, particularly when someone else can do it much better and faster.

In real estate investing, there are countless things that you simply *cannot* do as well as the professionals who go to school, train, get licensed, and practice every day in their field. You need those people on your team. You need the people who are superstars at what they do, people who do their job well, efficiently, and cost effectively, so that you can focus on the things that you do well, efficiently, and cost effectively. So, who goes on the team? Well, let's think about it.

The first and most obvious person to add to your team is what some call a bird dog. You need someone out in the field stirring up the business for you! If you can't find the houses to buy yourself, you need someone out there doing it for you. You could have one or a hundred bird dogs on your team, but at a minimum you should have a licensed real estate agent, specifically a hungry buyer's agent, willing to help you look for deals. You can network with multiple buyer's agents and make sure they all know you want to work with them. You can be sure they get paid on the acquisition side and, when you list your flip with them, they get paid on the disposition side, too. Network with wholesalers and others who are out in the field trying to find distressed properties and those that may make good investments. If you've got good bird dogs on your team, the deals will come to you!

You also need to have a particularly good seller's agent as well. When you find a great deal you want to flip, this agent is the one you'll plan to list the house with. Since they know you're listing it with them, they won't hesitate to run comps to be sure you're planning well along the way. The listing agent you choose needs to be someone with a good reputation in the community as someone who is trustworthy, easy to work with, and who gets top dollar for the homes they sell. This isn't always the same person as your buyer's agent, but it may be. If you have someone amazing, keep them close. If you don't have one yet, interview a dozen before you settle in on one.

Whether you are flipping, wholesaling, or buying rentals, you need a good contractor on your team. Ideally, you can find someone reliable that you call on as often as you get a deal. And, you keep them interested in your growth, keeping them busy with more projects. If you're using someone for the first time, tread lightly. There are a lot of ways things could go wrong. You'll do well to get referrals from people who have actually used the contractor you intend to hire, with good results. If you don't feel warm and fuzzy about them, don't use them. In a perfect world, you find a contractor you can use over and over, one who has subcontractors at his or her disposal in all of the trades. When you find the perfect contractor, let us know, though. We've been looking for that unicorn for years.

As you scale, you may want to add a project manager to your team, particularly if you already have a full-time job and can't check on your investment properties every day. A project manager can be especially useful when you have multiple projects going at once. You can spend your precious time on things that require more of you, perhaps your day job, acquisitions, or your family, while your project manager becomes the one who chases down the contractors and subcontractors to get the work done.

If you are acquiring real estate to put in a rental portfolio, you may be your own property manager at first. We strongly encourage you to consider adding a professional property management company to your team. This is another expense you may think you don't want to add to your cash flow analysis. However, if you factor in the value of your time, particularly after you have multiple units, you will soon find that the opportunity cost incurred by managing them yourself begins to grow rapidly. Moreover, the expense of the added stress is real—being the one responsible for all of the tenants, toilets, and termites is a heavy load, one we happily leave to the professionals. Interview several, check references, read reviews, and select the one (or more) that best fits the aim of your portfolio.

On the acquisition side, it helps also to have a stellar title company on your team. That is, you need to know that if you choose to close with a certain title company that they'll be there to help you get even the complicated deals to a closing table. Interview several and try them out one deal at a time. When you find ones you like working with, put them on the roster. You may find that some title companies are great for getting your run-of-the-mill flip listings to a closing table, while others are especially good at working with you on the acquisition side, particularly if you often buy with creative financing. Some, for instance, specialize in working with investors and are more familiar with seller financed deals and things that can be a little outside of the cookie-cutter deals. When you find the ones you know you can count on, keep them on your team.

Every house you get will need insurance. Long before you buy, you need to connect with a few insurance agents who can help you make sure your investments are covered. If you're buying in multiple geographical areas, you'll want someone on your team in each area. Since sometimes the deals can come quickly and need to close fast, you want a relationship with your insurance agents, who know what you're doing and who do their job well, so that you can get coverage as soon as you may need it. When you get good insurance agents on the team, it helps streamline the acquisition process as you continue to add doors to the portfolio.

Insurance agents are not the only professionals you need on your team, though. You are going to want a relationship with a good accountant and an experienced attorney. Specifically, you want an accountant and an attorney who are proficient and experienced in working with real estate investors. As an investor, your tax situation may get complicated pretty quickly. If you're used to using an online tax filing service, you should strongly consider adding a CPA to your team during the year you begin investing. If you've never hired an attorney before, it's time to bite the bullet. It's money well spent. Your lawyer can help you create or dissect contracts, create entities, evict trouble tenants, and help with any number of other legal issues you may have along the way. Spend some time interviewing quality candidates who are willing to do the work and put them on your team.

If you are planning to borrow money, you need to know where it's coming from, whether a banker or a hard money lender or both. There are countless hard money lenders who are looking to connect with people like you that want to invest in real estate. If you have the deal, it will not be difficult to find the money. Interview multiple lenders, get terms offered in writing, and keep your favorite hard money lenders handy. If you intend to bank more traditionally, whether through a mortgage broker or a commercial lender, you need a good banker—or several—who are willing to lend. Build a relationship with several banks in the areas in which you'll be investing, put money on deposit with their banks, get them your updated personal financial statement and last few years' taxes. Then, when you need them, they'll be ready, effectively competing with one another to make it on your team.

There are several other people that you could add to your team, but perhaps one of the most important is at least one experienced real estate investor who is willing to be your mentor and friend. "No man is an island." There is absolutely going to come a time when you want someone's opinion on a question in your mind, whether in deal analysis, investment strategy, reno estimate, tenant troubles, or any number of other issues you may face. You want someone that you can call. Take investor colleagues to lunch or coffee and gently pick their brain. Offer to help them in some way so you add value to what they're doing. Then, as you've built the relationship, when you need them, you'll be able to call upon them. Some of our best friendships have been made via real estate investing.

We can't leave this section without adding one more possible team member. If you have a spouse or significant other, remember you are not in this alone. If you have children that depend on you, you are not doing this for yourself alone. Your spouse or family may not be directly involved in the process of investing in real estate, perhaps, but they may need to be on the team. If you are buying real estate and spending tens or hundreds of thousands of dollars, perhaps even millions, you should involve your loved ones. If their input would be integral to making wise decisions, get it. If their future would be positively or detrimentally impacted by the results of your investments, involve them. If your sudden passing would leave someone else holding the bag, clueless as to what to do next, put them on your team. You owe it to your loved ones to take care of them in life and in death. Don't do any of this without them.

Key Point: You are not in this alone.

Notes

"I have no use for bodyguards, but I have very specific use for two highly trained, certified public accountants."

~Elvis Presley

CHAPTER 9: THE ENTITY

As you are thinking about your team, we thought this would be a good time to talk about entity structure. How you operate your investment business, how you take title to your investment properties, who guarantees a loan, and so many other things hinge on the answers to questions you don't yet know you should be asking. To reiterate, you need an accountant on your team who can properly advise you as to the tax consequences of operating in a particular fashion. You need an attorney on your team who can advise you the best ways to structure your investments to help you reach your goals while limiting your liability exposure. Nothing written here is intended to be a substitute for competent tax or legal advice and you should always rely on professionals licensed to practice in your area. However, there are a few general topics worthy of consideration here.

You could operate your investment business as a sole proprietorship. This, obviously, is one in which ownership is by and through a single person. Sole-proprietors own property in their own name and carry all of the weight on their shoulders.

Liability falls on them, individually, and there are few options by way of liability protection available (e.g. insurance, umbrella insurance, etc.). Your accountant may say that all of your income and expenses flow directly to your personal tax return. Your lawyer may say that you are most exposed when investing in your personal name. While this is probably the most common mechanism for doing business, this may or may not be the best route for you to take.

Anytime there are two or more people involved in a venture, it could be construed as a partnership. While the term partnership can be used in a number of ways, it is generally used in terms of general partnerships or limited partnerships. In a general partnership, all partners are presumed to be actively involved in the venture, while in a limited partnership, there may be limited/silent partners while one or more general partners are actively involved in the business. Talk to your accountant about the tax ramifications and possible additional filings necessary when operating as a partnership, such as a Partnership Tax Return. Your lawyer should be able to help craft the partnership agreements and other documents that may become necessary to outline roles of partners in the joint ventures. When taking title to properties with other people, you'll want to be very specific as to whether or not you are taking title as Tenants in Common or Joint Tenants. This is another question for the lawyer on your team.

You have probably heard of or perhaps even own a Limited Liability Company. These entities are formed to allow people to create a business, such as real estate investment holding companies, and have statutory limits to liability while engaging in business as the LLC. We won't get too deep, to address member-managed versus manager-managed and so forth, because your attorney and/or CPA can best advise you on what works for you in your jurisdiction. But we have to comment on the real beauty of the LLC, the limitation of liability. An LLC and its holdings are generally protected from judgments arising from matters occurring outside of the LLC and anything you hold outside the LLC is generally protected from judgments arising from matters occurring inside of the LLC. There are exceptions, such as when a Plaintiff manages to "pierce the corporate veil," but this is why you have a great CPA and attorney on your team; to help you design the best entity structure for you.

Your accountant or attorney may tell you that you should form a Corporation, whether a C-Corp or an S-Corp. The pros and cons of incorporating are far too great for us to get into here, but they are worthy of study. A C-Corp involves ownership of one or more shareholders, which could be either individuals or other entities. An S-Corp can be owned by estates, trust, individuals, or entities, even tax-exempt entities. We are beginning to sound like a broken record when we say this but check with the CPA and attorney on your team and see what makes the most sense for you in your situation.

> **Key Point:** Your accountant and attorney are likely well-equipped to help you structure your real estate investment in the manner most advantageous to you.

You may also benefit from looking into setting up one or more trusts for your investment business. When a property is owned in trust there is a trustee who has a fiduciary obligation to tend to the asset for the benefit of the true owner, the beneficiary. The trustee and the beneficiary are not necessarily the same person or entity. It may very well be that your estate planning needs may be best met by investing in real estate held in trust, for the benefit of your heirs, depending on your financial planning goals. Once again, talk to your lawyer and your accountant before making plans to create a trust.

Whatever entity structure you choose, make that choice based on good research and even better advice, and be flexible. Some of your investments may best be suited for a particular entity structure while others may not. For instance, we may want to own something as partners as joint tenants (or tenants by the entirety) with a right of survivorship. However, our friend Steve may want to own a piece of investment property with us together as Tenants in Common. With a true partnership, you may have to file a Partnership Tax Return and its necessary forms, while a Limited Co-Ownership Agreement may make you and your joint venturer separate enough that a Partnership Return is not required. Be sure you are always protecting yourself, protecting your family, and protecting your asset. Then you'll be just fine.

Notes

"The greater the obstacle, the more glory in overcoming it."

~ Molière

CHAPTER 10: THE CHALLENGE

Oh, the challenges you will face—they are many. We wish we could tell you that real estate investing is all fun and games, but it is truly challenging. Rarely a week goes by that our project manager doesn't repeat "if it was easy, everyone would be doing it." Sometimes it is hard; sometimes it is very hard. It is taxing on your body and mind. It is taxing on your time and energy. It is taxing on your relationships. And it might just be taxing on your financial situation, resulting in just the opposite of the intended result.

We've said that the hardest part about real estate investing is finding the deal. That may very well be true, but it is certainly not the only hard part. As you begin your efforts toward becoming a net worth millionaire through real estate investing, you will face innumerable challenges along the way. There are far too many to summarize in one chapter, here, but we hope this serves as an opportunity to keep your feet on the ground. The fact of the matter is that not everyone who plays the game wins. Just as you've heard that most small businesses fail, many who long to invest in real estate face challenges that appear, or perhaps are, insurmountable.

First of all, there are inner challenges. There is—and should be—an inner struggle where you are forced to balance desires and objectives across multiple facets of life. You want to invest in real estate, but you don't want to put your family's financial future at too much risk. You know that borrowing money to invest in real estate can increase your return on investment, but you don't want to sink the ship, going too far into debt. You must balance the interests of life, work, family, friends, mental health, risk of substance abuse, and so many other things in order to overcome these inner challenges.

If you have a history of depression, anxiety, risk of suicide, mental health issues, substance abuse issues, or the like, tread extremely carefully. If you suffer from any form of addiction or have a propensity to move too quickly, making abrupt decisions without collecting all of the facts, it is especially important that you have an accountability partner to help keep you in check. If your marriage is already at risk, perhaps because you *work too much*, don't become so obsessed with real estate, as is so easy to do, such that it costs you your marriage or family.

If you struggle with greed, covetousness, or dishonesty, you have some inner challenges that must be overcome before you ever set foot into business, whether real estate investing or otherwise. No matter how many doors you have, it will never be enough. No matter how much money you'll make, you may do whatever it takes to make more, even to others' disadvantage. This is simply not how to get far in real estate, business, or life. Overcome these inner challenges and *then* let's look at investing in real estate for the benefit of yourself, your family, and your community.

The outward challenges are more obvious, though not necessarily more important to recognize. We just see those more easily. There will be people who lie to you, cheat you, steal from you, talk bad about you behind your back, and otherwise do you harm. When you think you have an all-star team of reputable, honest, intelligent, and generous team members, one of them will let you down in a big way. Your contractor may have fallen on hard times and decide to inflate a bid to steal a little bit more money on the deal. Your realtor, bound by professional rules of ethical conduct, may neglect to send you a higher offer because the one they want you to accept nets them both sides of a commission. Your banker, your property manager, your project manager, and everyone else on your team is human. We all fail. We all make mistakes. We all let each other down at one time or another.

While you may try to operate your investment business at the highest level of integrity, there will always be people who fail to appreciate your desire to reach for such a standard. Perhaps believing that such a height is unreachable, some do not even bother to try. Some will take a deposit on work to be done and simply never show up to the job site. Some will promise to pay you a referral or give you first shot at a deal then disappear when the time comes to do what is right. These outward challenges are some we face at almost every turn and in every deal. They weigh heavily on us, knowing the hundreds of thousands of dollars that others have cost us over the years—money that could have gone to far greater causes than to line the pockets of the ones who took advantage of us. But it allows us to share this with you, here. Know that these challenges are very real and be wary.

Some say the greatest challenge they face in real estate is when they lose money on a deal. It is particularly relevant for discussion if you're considering investing for the first time and, perhaps, do not have the cushion to sustain missing the mark on a deal. If you run numbers on a flip that will net you $20k, but you missed the ARV by $15k and the reno by another $15k, you quickly just lost $10,000 on the deal. If you buy a house to rent and the margins are already thin, what happens when the HVAC goes out in the first month, which has happened to us far too many times? That several thousand-dollar hit may be a tough one to swallow when it comes.

The financial challenge of losing money on a deal can be a hard one to overcome, but there is a glass-half-full way of looking at it. If you work through the process of putting a team together, finding a property, buying the property, renovating the property, flipping or renting the property, and it ultimately does not go well, financially, you probably learned a ton along the way. If you learned every step of the way, finding your strengths and weaknesses, figuring out what works and doesn't work, cutting people from the team that don't need to be there and adding the people that do, what is that worth? If you lost ten grand, did you get ten grand worth of education? (If you went to college, what did that education cost you?) You get to take that education with you to the next deal, build on it, and continue to grow! More than one investor has said that losing money is the best way to learn how to invest in real estate.

> **Key Point:** Losing money on a deal is unfortunate, but there is an optimistic approach you can take to absorbing the impact of any loss. Everything is a learning opportunity and a chance to grow.

There are numerous other challenges you can and will face, perhaps the most stressful being when someone accuses you of doing something wrong, whether intentionally or negligently, and perhaps even taking you to court. Remember that in real estate investing, as with any business, you are dealing with humans. And some humans are just plain terrible. Even when you try to hold yourself to the highest standard of excellence in your business, something stupid may happen and someone will hate you for it, blaming you until the day they die. People will say evil things about you, may be jealous of your success and try to thwart it, and some will try to take away from you and what you're doing—but keep your head up and your eyes on prize. *Always do the right thing* and know that the finish line is worth the pain of running the race.

Notes

*If you got a chance, take it, take it while you got a chance.
If you got a dream, chase it, 'cause a dream won't chase you back.*

~Cody Johnson

CHAPTER 11: THE DREAM

All this time we've spent so far, we've talked about getting you to The First Million. It may seem like a lofty goal, building a net worth of over a million dollars through strategic investments in real estate. Perhaps it feels surreal to think that you really can make it happen. Perhaps it feels unattainable at times, yet at other times you pursue it with far more confidence. What we want you to realize, though, is that the dream addressed thus far is merely The *First* Million. There is a world of good that you can do as you pursue the heights of, and then far beyond, The First Million. What do you want to do?

We think it is healthy to dream. Some people simply operate better when there is a carrot on the end of the stick held in front of them. We think you should set goals, like we talked about early on. Dream about what you'd like to accomplish in life and business. Write those dreams down and pursue them. It is healthy to try to make the most of your situation, and if your circumstances, environment, opportunities, and skillset afford you the ability to become a net worth millionaire, go for it! Dream. Dream big.

Think about the good that you can do if you live below your means, pay off the weight of consumer debt, invest in your future, and become a magnificent financial blessing to your family and the community around you.

Dream.
Could you, through education, diligence, perseverance, and strategic planning set yourself up in such a way that you don't have to work a job that no longer brings you joy?

Dream.
If you were able to capitalize on opportunities around you now in such a way that in a matter of years money was no longer an issue, would you take it upon yourself to put a roof over the head of a needy family, put someone else's children through college, or buy a car for that struggling single mother down the street?

Dream big.
If your goal is to become financially free so that you can help bear the burden of others, I genuinely don't want you to stop at The First Million. The key word there is "first." The implication is that there will be a second, third, tenth, and beyond. If you can put together the plan to get your financial habits on track and put your real estate education to use, The First Million won't be the last. You will have laid a foundation on which you can continue to build. Your portfolio will continue to appreciate, your amortized loans will continue to reduce their principal balance, and your rents will, hopefully, keep going up. As you look to seize more and more opportunities, those already seized will continue to build, compounding on one another over time.

Wealth building can feel like an unstoppable, runaway train. When the train is getting started, it takes an immense amount of energy to get it moving. Even still, it takes a long time to get the train up to speed. If the analogy persists, it's like trying to get that train up the mountain carrying a multitude of heavily loaded cars along the way, with much difficulty. But once that train reaches a certain point, as if cresting the mountain to begin its path back down, all of that weight and energy is now back in its favor. All of that potential energy, gravity, weight, and momentum hurl that runaway train down the tracks and virtually nothing can stand in its way!

Dream.

> **Key Point:** Wealth building can feel like an unstoppable runaway train. Once it reaches a certain level of momentum, it begins to feel like it happens automatically, and nothing can stand in its way.

You may feel as if the beginning of your real estate journey is too heavy a load to bear, the journey too long, the way too difficult, or you are ill-equipped, not having enough energy or momentum. Just put one foot in front of the other. Hunger and thirst for education and wisdom. Keep putting one foot in front of the other. Seize the opportunities that come your way. Keep stepping in the right direction. Build on your strengths and your failures as you continue to push forward, climbing that mountain.

Then, at some point, you'll look back and see that you've flipped or wholesaled a handful of houses. You've bought, renovated, refinanced, and kept in your rental portfolio a handful of doors that are appreciating and cash flowing. You'll update your personal financial statement to show that you've eliminated a handful of debts and liabilities, replacing them with good debt and assets in which you hold equity. You'll run the numbers and see exactly what you've been hoping for, The First Million. Then you'll save your spreadsheet, close out of the app, and get right back to work.

The train keeps on going. The assets in your portfolio continue to appreciate, because you bought them in areas that are thriving and postured for growth. They cash flow and that cash flow is increasing, because you bought in good school zones where rents continue to climb. The equity spread continues to grow because you financed those rentals in a way that dramatically increases your return on investment while forcibly multiplying your net worth. While you sleep, The First Million keeps working for you. While you work on building your portfolio even further, The First Million works even harder. While you look for ways to serve your family and the community around you, The First Million keeps serving you and those you serve. While you dream of what's next, The First Million makes that dream come sooner than you ever thought possible.

That's the dream. Keep dreaming big. When you do hit that goal of *The First Million*, you'll be ready for what's next. *The Next Million.*

Notes

"Don't wait to buy real estate. Buy real estate and wait."
~Will Rogers

CONCLUSION

Answer this question honestly. What's holding you back? The time is now to begin putting wheels in motion. The time is now to begin putting these tools in your tool belt and for you to get to work. The time is now to put the energy into accomplishing what you know in your heart you can accomplish. You know your *why*; you know what to do; now do it. What's holding you back?

As we began, we considered the volume and variety of emotions that must be going through your head and heart as you look down this path. You've done well, sticking with us through to the end of the book. We know the emotions have multiplied and your response to what you've learned may be many. Perhaps you are afraid, intimidated by the fear of the unknown. Perhaps you are overwhelmed by the amount of learning you still need in order to be successful.

One thing is for sure, you can do it. We've truly skimmed the surface talking about such a deep subject, real estate investing. We only lightly touched on countless subjects and terms that may have been—and still are—foreign to you. You don't have to know exactly how a wraparound mortgage works or how to explain a contract for deed, yet. You just need to get started. Along the journey, always be learning. Dig deep and research like crazy. Find and listen to a mentor. Study at the feet of those who have done what you want to do, online and in person. Just get started.

The most important step in any journey is the first one. Take that first step. You may trip. You may fall. But your journey will have begun. Remember that "Rome wasn't built in a day," and there is a long way to go. But you can do it. Do it.

Made in the USA
Columbia, SC
17 April 2024